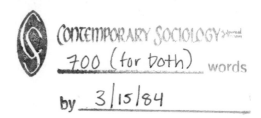

CONTEMPORARY SOCIOLOGY

700 (for both) words

by 3/15/84

84

The Kula

A bibliography

The Kula

A bibliography

MARTHA MACINTYRE

CAMBRIDGE UNIVERSITY PRESS

CAMBRIDGE

LONDON   NEW YORK   NEW ROCHELLE

MELBOURNE   SYDNEY

Published by the Press Syndicate of the University of Cambridge
The Pitt Building, Trumpington Street, Cambridge CB2 1RP
32 East 57th Street, New York, NY 10022, USA
296 Beaconsfield Parade, Middle Park, Melbourne 3206, Australia

First published 1983

Printed in Great Britain at
the University Press, Cambridge

Library of Congress catalogue card number: 82–4142

British Library Cataloguing in Publication Data

Macintyre, Martha
The Kula : a bibliography
1. Economics, Primitive–Papua New Guinea
–Bibliography   2. Barter–Bibliography
I. Title
016.381'0995'3   ZS118.E25

ISBN 0 521 23203 1

MU

Contents

Acknowledgements

In preparing this bibliography, I have incurred many debts. The following people assisted me by providing details of items which I could not trace in the libraries available to me in England: Fred Damon; Raymond Firth; Susan Gardner; Peter Gathercole; Jack Golson; Paul Jorion; Peter Lauer; John Liep; Susan Montague; Nancy Munn; Andrej Paluch; Harold Scheffler; Erhard Schlesier; Giancarlo Scoditti; Carl Thune; Annette Weiner and Michael Young. Jerry Leach assisted in the compilation throughout and must be acknowledged as the major collaborator of the kula bibliography. The British S.S.R.C. provided the initial grant for research and Sir Edmund Leach provided generous financial help which allowed for the completion of the bibliography and enabled me to travel to various museums in England to study the collections. Murdoch University provided finance for travel to Australian museums. I am grateful to the many museum curators who went to great pains to supply details of the collections of Massim artefacts. Shirley Prendergast and Leonie Pimm assisted me in the final checking and manuscript preparation. Any errors are of course my own responsibility. I would like to express my gratitude to Sir Edmund Leach for his encouragement and support, both personal and intellectual, while I was preparing the kula bibliography.

Introduction

This bibliography is designed to be both a work of reference and stimulus to research. It is also a reminder of Bronislaw Malinowski's influence as an anthropologist, since it documents the response to *The Argonauts of the Western Pacific* over the past fifty-six years. The kula as an institution, and the theoretical insights which Malinowski developed in his attempt to explain it, have provided food for thought for generations of anthropologists and this comprehensive bibliography of the kula reflects the course of development of social anthropology in Britain and America throughout this period.

The bibliography was originally conceived simply as a background document for the Kula Conference held at Kings' College, Cambridge, in July 1978, but like all such projects, the objectives have altered as the work progressed. I had originally envisaged a reference work, mainly concerned with Malinowski's and other anthropologists' interpretations of the kula. However, it was intended from the start to include a catalogue of general textbook references to the kula, some of which are, by now, far removed from any factual ethnography either of the past or the present. Knowledge of the workings of the kula is nowadays a standard requirement for undergraduates studying Social or Cultural Anthropology but it is the kula of textbook writers rather than the kula as understood by Malinowski that has thus attained a mythic identity in the History of Anthropology. This bibliography traces that development. In this way it is a resource not only for the ethnographic specialist but for the historian of Social Anthropology. I. Jarvie states firmly in his analysis of British anthropological thought that ' ... functionalism was generated by the peculiarities of the Trobriand kula ...' (p. 183) and Claude Lévi-Strauss is equally convinced that Mauss' theoretical genius in analyzing the kula provided the basis for the emergence of structuralist theory (*The Scope of Anthropology*, Cape, 1967, p. 13). This bibliography provides the means of evaluating such generalizations.

The bibliography also brings together a great variety of pre-Malinowskian observations of the kula and other trading activities in the Massim area. These are unsystematic accounts in Government publications; unpublished Patrol

1

Reports; Mission Records; popular travel books and memoirs. There are also the more recent items of recorded oral history made by individuals from the region. Malinowski himself recognized that the kula had undergone a series of transformations since the late nineteenth century but this historical insight did not really affect his analysis. But latterly, the work of anthropologist R.F. Salisbury, of historian Hank Nelson and archaeologists J. Allen and Jack Golson has been a stimulus for the development of an historical approach to the study of trade and exchange systems of New Guinea. The ethnographic descriptions which crop up in missionaries', and colonists' memoirs, or as incidental information in the settlement of a dispute over property attain a new relevance in the light of anthropological research and new archaeological interests. The material is voluminous and often difficult to categorize. Some of the writers were racist or condescending in their attitudes towards the societies and customs they observed, others painstakingly recorded native institutions with sensitivity and humility. The observations of Resident Magistrates such as R. Bellamy on the Trobriands or A.P. Lyons on Woodlark Island provide invaluable information about Massim societies during a period of economic change which had a profound effect on inter-island trade and exchange relations. The A.P. Lyons papers, which are deposited in the Fryer Memorial Library, University of Queensland, contain many drawings and explanations of artefacts and technological processes he collected and observed. This material could extend our limited knowledge of Massim material culture which, to date, is drawn mainly from the hastily gathered observations of Seligmann and the scrutiny of the objects which he and others collected. Though such material is ultimately relevant to our theme, an indiscriminate inclusion of historical sources would have opened the floodgates, and for this reason we have only included works which mention some aspect of trade or production which can be directly related to kula exchange. The Polynesian Society's *A Pacific Bibliography* by C.R.H. Taylor and the bibliographies in *Canoes of Oceania* by A. Haddon and J. Hornell, *Black, White and Gold* by Hank Nelson and the Australian National University's ethnographic bibliography of Papua New Guinea *An Ethnographic Bibliography of New Guinea*, ANU Press, 1968 (two volumes), provide detailed information on primary and secondary historical material on the Massim.

As an example of an anecdotal work by a thoroughly prejudiced European observer, which nevertheless has value for historical purposes, I have included Beatrice Grimshaw's book *The New New Guinea* (see item 90). She briefly refers to 'markets in native jewellery' in the area and a 'native syndicate' but includes enough description to make it clear that she is presenting a garbled version of the kula. Despite her general contempt for native customs, she reaches the conclusion that kula valuables are comparable with European 'historical diamonds', foreshadowing Malinowski's 'crown jewels' analogy by more than ten years! More importantly, she provides confirmation for many of Seligmann's and

Malinowski's statements about the exchange of valuables. For example, she notes that *mwali* circulate in pairs; she gives approximate values for *mwali* in Australian currency in 1890, which are surprisingly consistent with those recorded by Seligmann and other European collectors who purchased *mwali* during the 1900–1910 period; she reveals that white employers used *mwali* as wages for native labour and that a trader resident on Rossel Island had instituted a 'mint' on a small scale, where he employed his indentured labourers making *sapi-sapi*. These fragments of ethnographic information and details of colonial intervention in native economic systems obviously vary in quality, reliability and details, but when interpreted in the light of other research, often provide crucial insights into the nature and development of Massim exchange over the period of colonization.

Another aspect of kula history which is illuminated by the material in this bibliography is the relationship between ceremonial exchange and the trade exchange of objects of common utility. Malinowski made an absolute distinction between the two forms of exchange and insisted that the kula itself had wholly non-utilitarian functions. Whether Malinowski's observations really justified this view may be disputed but my bibliographic evidence at least suggests that the kula which Malinowski observed in 1916 may have been very different from the kula of 1906 or 1896 or 1886. H.H. Romilly's *The Western Pacific and New Guinea* includes acute observations on the economic interdependence of the Laughlans and Woodlark Island. He describes an inter-island trade in canoes and stone implements, but then states categorically that the activities of a single trader in the area have ensured the wide-spread use of steel axes, so that in 1886 he believes 'the age of stone has vanished'. In 1906 Seligmann observed that the quarries at Suloga on Woodlark Island had not been worked for two generations (see item 480). The ceremonial function of stone axe blades noted by Malinowski was not necessarily a recent innovation, but the absence of utilitarian axe heads certainly was recent and this must have altered the context in which *vaygua* axe heads were exchanged.

It is, of course, impossible to reconstruct, with any certainty, the social context of prehistoric exchange and it is only recently that archaeologists have begun to speculate on the patterns and circumstances of pre-historic trade in the Massim. The section of the bibliography dealing with the archaeology of the kula contains some of the most interesting recent research on exchange systems in the area. Early archaeological studies focussed almost exclusively on the mysterious stone structures which can be found on several islands. Recent work by Egloff (see item 554), Irwin (see item 309), and Lauer (see items 337–339, 566) has challenged anthropological assumptions about the immutability and geographical limits of the kula and other similar trading systems. These three writers have concentrated on the production and distribution of pottery throughout the area, postulating the coincidence of pottery routes with the kula 'ring'. Lauer argues that his archaeological evidence on changing patterns in the pottery trade suggest equally extensive changes in ceremonial exchange and that the apparent economic irrationality of the kula is the result of changes brought about by colonial pacification and trade. Analysis to date has been undertaken in terms of trade in durable items such as pottery, stone tools and obsidian rather than the shell ornaments which in historic times have constituted the essential kula exchange. The relationship between kula and other trade has long been a focus for anthropological debate and the conclusions reached by archaeologists concerning the kula and its earlier social functions may well regenerate those arguments. But it would be artificial to propose that the co-operative research projects implied by many of the questions recently raised by both anthropologists and archaeologists necessarily bridge the theoretical and methodological differences between the two disciplines. This bibliography provides the basis for the development of interdisciplinary research in the Massim area.

The literature on the art of the Massim has a long tradition, beginning with Haddon's *The Decorative Art of British New Guinea: A Study in Papuan Ethnography* published in 1894 (see item 595). It has been generally acknowledged that the carving and painting of Trobriand craftsmen is superior to the work of other islanders and European scholars and collectors have concentrated on the Trobriands in their assessments of Massim art. However, stylistic homogeneity, which can be related directly to patterns of inter-island contact through trade, may have resulted in inaccuracies of attribution (see D. Newton, *Massim, Art of the Massim Area, New Guinea*, item 606) and there is still much to be explored in this field which can throw light on exchange. One of the essential elements of the kula is that it is the concrete expression of aesthetic and artistic values. The Massim ideals of beauty are constantly expounded in kula myth and magic, the articles exchanged are valued precisely because of their intrinsic beauty, in form, colour, texture and sound. Malinowski initially referred to these aesthetic issues in Trobriand culture but more recent anthropological study has extended the scope of such inquiry. The work of Nancy Munn on Gawa, Shirley Campbell on Vakuta, Giancarlo Scoditti on Kitava and most particularly Annette Weiner on Kiriwina has demonstrated forcefully the importance of research into the production and aesthetic assessment of Massim art. In the context of such discussions much is revealed about the circumstances of production and the aims of the craftsmen which can be related to general issues in the study of trade and exchange as redistribution in the area. It is clear from collections, and observations by travellers and anthropologists that the production of works of art for trade has been a feature of the Massim economy for a considerable period.

Several films have been made on the Trobriands, two of which have received awards as examples of ethnographic cinematography. The kula has featured in most of these and they, therefore, constitute a valuable source for the non-fieldworker. Even where the ethnographic value is minimal, because kula practice was abandoned for the sake of clarity in the film maker's terms, the films still

4

convey striking visual images of Massim life and of the kula objects themselves. Annette Weiner's critical article 'Epistemology and Ethnographic Reality: A Trobriand Island Case Study' (see item 527) is the only comprehensive anthropological appraisal of the films of the kula.

In compiling the bibliography, I excluded articles which mentioned the kula only incidentally while discussing other aspects of Trobriand or Massim society or culture. For example, in 1932 Malinowski, Rentoul and others debated on the Trobriand ideas of physiological paternity in the pages of *MAN*. They referred to the kula in passing but usually only to suggest a common activity in the Massim. The published debates about Trobriand beliefs on paternity did not illuminate any aspect of the kula and for that reason I decided to exclude them. Initially, I made the same judgement about Leach's and Austen's items on Trobriand calendrical systems; however, recent work in other areas on native systems of measurement involving the seasons and the stars and a speculative unpublished paper by Fred Damon has caused me to revise this and I have included them, although in themselves they offer no information on the kula or any other trade.

There is also a considerable body of literature related to Trobriand kinship systems and social hierarchy. In only a few of the articles on these subjects is the kula discussed. I have included only those which refer to the ways in which kinship is related to kula activities or which discuss the kula in respect to rank and hierarchy, such as the articles on chieftainship by Brunton (see item 174) and Salisbury (see item 457).

Unpublished papers and sources have provided me with the usual bibliographer's headaches. The library at the Australian National University in Canberra has substantial holdings of unpublished materials gathered from institutional and personal sources. Many of these are on microfilm. The Malinowski papers are divided between the Sterling Memorial Library at Yale University and the British Library of Political and Economic Science at the London School of Economics. A detailed catalogue is available for the Yale set. The BLPES papers are being catalogued at present; the archivist will provide information. Where people have indicated their preparedness to give access to unpublished papers, I have included them in the bibliography; the microfilms and tapes collected by Jerry Leach during his fieldwork are available to other researchers as are the unpublished articles by F. Damon and N. Munn. Given constraints of time and money, the tracing and annotation of unpublished material in any comprehensive fashion was impossible.

The bibliography is divided into subject categories which are very broad and refer to form and content. The first section comprises all the relevant work of Bronislaw Malinowski and is only annotated in terms of pinpointing incidental references in works other than *The Argonauts of the Western Pacific* (see item 7). The second section covers unpublished primary material. Section three deals with historical and pre-Malinowskian references to kula and trade in the Massim. Section four constitutes the body of the bibliography and consists of anthropological books, articles, unpublished theses and papers in English and several other languages. Archaeological references are in section five, art and aesthetics in section six, and films in section seven.

Within each section entries are arranged alphabetically and chronologically, according to author. I have avoided cross-references except where it seemed academically useful, for example, where a scholarly commentary or criticism has altered the importance of an article, such as M. Young's discussion of Bromilow (see item 121) which enriches the value of the original material (see item 80). Cross-referencing is facilitated by the numbering of each entry, which is sequential, and for the purpose of tracing items through the author index.

Annotations have been kept as brief as possible and are intended to outline the relevance of the item for a study of the kula. I have only attempted a summary of content or argument where the whole article is concerned with kula or other trade. I have not indicated specific page references for every item. Those without page references are usually items which are entirely focussed on the kula, so that no single page is usefully isolated for reference, for example, the article by W. Sloan (see item 485); or alternatively when the reference to exchange is so general or theoretical that it is misleading to give specific page references to mention of the kula, as in the articles by Godelier (see item 259) and Sahlins (see items items 451 and 455).

So that items can be traced easily, I have included the publisher's name and place of publication – the few entries which lack this information were included on the advice of anthropologists who sent entries but neglected to include those details. Sometimes I was informed of a reference but was unable to trace it; sometimes I would track down a rare book in a library, only to discover that it was missing on a subsequent visit for the purpose of annotation! These problems are reflected in omissions and incomplete entries. As the purpose of the bibliography is to aid research and stimulate informed debate, I decided that it was preferable to include these entries and offer them in a spirit of intellectual inquiry, rather than exclude them to conform to pedagogical standards of completeness.

It was not until the bibliography project was well under way that I became aware of the abundance of Massim artefacts relating to the kula which exists in museums throughout the world. The decision to include a directory to these museums created many problems and eventually the constraints of time and money prevailed, so that the information included is minimal. There are a few collections of Massim material culture which do not hold the important kula objects, but which have numerous items exchanged in the context of the kula. Unfortunately, I was unaware of the complexity of kula exchanges involving other other items when I began the museum survey, so I may have excluded a few relevant museums.

Bronislaw Malinowski on the *Kula*

Malinowski's *Argonauts of the Western Pacific* has been through seven impressions and, in 1978, was first published as a paperback by Routledge and Kegan Paul. It has been translated and published in several other languages but details were not easy to obtain: however, Helena Malinowska informed me that she knew of a Spanish translation which was published by Ediciones 62; a Portuguese language edition by Abril in Brazil; and another in Serbo-Croatian by B.I.G. Zavod.

1. Malinowski, Bronislaw (n.d.) (unpublished) Collected Papers. Most of Malinowski's papers, notebooks, letters, lectures, etc. have been deposited in the London School of Economics Library. At the time of compilation they are still uncatalogued and are, therefore, unavailable. It should be noted, however, that Malinowski's field notebooks are almost incomprehensible to anyone not conversant in English, Polish and German. Another collection is held in the Library at Yale University; this has been catalogued in detail.
2. Malinowski, Bronislaw (1915) 'The Natives of Mailu', in *Proceedings of the Royal Society of South Australia*, Vol. 39. Published by the Society, Adelaide, see especially pp. 592-646. This is an important work both in terms of its ethnographical information and as a source for understanding Malinowski's theoretical interests and the development of his fieldwork methodology. Chapter IV, 'Economics', contains valuable information on trade, value, production and distribution on Mailu. There is a description of the production of armshells and other shell ornaments.
3. Malinowski, Bronislaw (1918) 'Fishing in the Trobriand Islands', in *MAN*, XVIII, Article 53, pp. 87-92. Marginal, of use to compare rituals surrounding fishing with those of kula.
4. Malinowski, Bronislaw (1920) 'War and Weapons among the Natives of the Trobriand Islands', in *MAN*, Article 5, January, 1920, pp. 10-12. Dis-

cusses the way in which certain artefacts are ceremonial rather than utilitarian in their main uses. A brief presentation of the nature of Trobriand warfare.

5. Malinowski, Bronislaw (1920) 'Kula: The circulating exchanges of valuables in the Archipelagos of Eastern New Guinea', in *MAN*, Vol. XX, Article 51, pp. 97–105. Malinowski's first description of the kula. The map and some of his statements on the valuables are worth comparing with the *Argonauts* as there are significant differences. Reprinted in part in *Tribal and Peasant Economies. Readings in Economic Anthropology*, Dalton, G. (ed.) (1967) (see item 206).

6. Malinowski, Bronislaw (1921) 'The Primitive Economics of the Trobriand Islanders', in *The Economic Journal*, Vol. XXXI, London, pp. 1 - 16. Reprinted in 1970 in *Cultures of the Pacific*, Harding, T.G. & Wallace, B.J. (eds.) (see item 274).

7. Malinowski, Bronislaw (1922) *Argonauts of the Western Pacific. An Account of Native Enterprise and Adventure in the Archipelagoes of Melanesian New Guinea*. Routledge & Kegan Paul, London. Chapter VI reprinted in *Tribal and Peasant Economies. Readings in Economic Anthropology*, Dalton, G. (ed.) (1967) (see item 206).

8. Malinowski, Bronislaw (1924) 'Complex and Myth in Mother-right', in *Psyche*, Vol. V, No. 1, July, 1924. Not seen by editor.

9. Malinowski, Bronislaw (1925) 'Magic, Science and Religion', in *Science, Religion and Reality*, Needham, J. (ed.). The Sheldon Press, London. No direct reference to the kula, but constant reference to Melanesian fieldwork. Outlines theoretical basis for the study of primitive institutions involving obligations and co-operation.

10. Malinowski, Bronislaw (1926) *Crime and Custom in Savage Society*. Routledge & Kegan Paul, London (International Library of Psychology, Philosophy and Scientific Method), pp. 26, 61, 82, 90, 104, 110. Discussion of reciprocity as a coercive element in the establishment of 'legal' relationships – kula usually used as an example.

11. Malinowski, Bronislaw (1927) *Sex and Repression in Savage Society*. Routledge & Kegan Paul, London, pp. 93–94, 130. Refers to dreams and magic relating to kula activities.

12. Malinowski, Bronislaw (1927) 'Lunar and Seasonal Calendar in the Trobriands', in *Journal of the Royal Anthropological Institute*, LXII, pp. 203-215.

13. Malinowski, Bronislaw (1929) 'Spirit-hunting in the South Seas', in *The Realist*, Vol. II, 1929, pp. 398–417, especially p. 406.

14. Malinowski, Bronislaw (1929) *The Sexual Life of Savages in North-Western Melanesia*. G. Routledge & Sons Ltd., London, pp. 22, 30, 36, 50, 77, 81, 97, 213–216, 220, 245, 271, 291, 328–330, 383, 415. Trobriand sexual

roles and practices in connection with kula. In this work, Malinowski appears to use kula as a generic term for all ceremonial exchange (see pp. 97 and 215).

15. Malinowski, Bronislaw (n.d. [1929]) *Das Geschlechtsleben der Wilden in Nordwest-Melanesien*. Vorwort von H. Ellis, Übersetzung von E. Schumann. Grethlein und Co., Leipzig and Zurich.

16. Malinowski, Bronislaw (1929) 'Practical Anthropology', in *Africa*, Vol. II, London, pp. 23-39. See especially section on Primitive Economics.

17. Malinowski, Bronislaw (1930, 1970) *La vie sexuelle des sauvages du Nord-Ouest de la Mélanésie*. (Trad. de L'anglais par S. Jankélévitch.) Payot, Paris

18. Malinowski, Bronislaw (1932) *La sexualité et sa répression dans les sociétés primitives*. (Trad. de l'anglais par S. Jankélévitch.) Payot, Paris. New edition 1967.

19. Malinowski, Bronislaw (1933) *Moeurs et coutumes des Mélanésiens*. (Trad. de l'anglais par S. Jankélévitch.) Payot, Paris. Reprinted in 1968 under new title: *Trois essais sur la vie sociale des primitifs*.

20. Malinowski, Bronislaw (1934) 'Stone Implements in Eastern New Guinea', in *Essays Presented to Seligmann*, Evans Pritchard, E.E. et al. (eds.). Kegan Paul, Trench, Trubner & Co. Ltd., London, pp. 189-196. Discusses the manufacture and uses of stone implements, giving details on *beku*, those usually traded in the kula.

21. Malinowski, Bronislaw (1935) *Coral Gardens and Their Magic*. A Study of the Methods of Tilling the Soil and of Agricultural Rites in the Trobriand Islands. Vol. 1, The Description of Gardening; Vol. 2, The Language of Magic and Gardening. George Allen & Unwin Ltd., London. Volume I contains brief references to the kula on pp. 74, 294 and Appendix II contains Malinowski's acknowledgement of some theoretical inadequacies of his analysis of the kula.

22. Malinowski, Bronislaw (1939) 'The Group and the Individual in Functional Analysis', in *American Journal of Sociology,* Vol. XLIV.

23. Malinowski, Bronislaw (1940) *Sitte und Verbrechen bei den Natürvolken*. Übersetzung von H. Schwarz. Sammlung Dalp. Bd. 33, Bern.

24. Malinowski, Bronislaw & de la Fuente, Julio (1941) *La Economía de un Sistema de Mercados en México. Un Ensayo de Etnografía Contemporánea y Cambio Social en un Valle Mexicano* (The Economics of a Mexican Market System. An Essay in Contemporary Ethnography and Social Change in a Mexican Valley), in *Acta Anthropologica*, Epoca 2, vol. I, no. 3. Escuela Nacional de Antropología e Historia. Sociedad de Alumnos, Mexico, 1957.

25. Malinowski, Bronislaw (1959) *Crime and Custom in Savage Society*. Littlefield, Adams & Co., Paterson, New Jersey. (American edition.)

The Kula: a bibliography

26. Malinowski, Bronislaw (1962) *Geschlechtstreib und Verdrängung bei den Primitiven.* Übersetzung von Hugo Steinfeld. Reihe 'Rowohlts Deutsche Enzyklopädie' Bd. 139/140, Reinbeck.
27. Malinowski, Bronislaw (1963) *Les Argonautes du Pacifique occidental.* (Trad. de l'anglais par A. & S. Deuijver.) Gallimard, Paris.
28. Malinowski, Bronislaw (1967) 'Kula' (1920) and 'Tribal Economics in the Trobriands' (Chapter VI, Divisions II - VI of *Argonauts*). Reprinted in *Tribal and Peasant Economies. Readings in Economic Anthropology*, Dalton, G. (ed.) (1967) (see item 206).
29. Malinowski, Bronislaw (1967) *A Diary in the Strict Sense of the Term.* London, pp. 118, 124. Not particularly informative, but contains hints of some of Malinowski's sources on the kula; passing references to Massim islands in terms of their involvement with kula trade.
30. Malinowski, Bronislaw (1968) Excerpts from: *Argonauts of the Western Pacific.* Routledge & Kegan Paul, London. Reprinted in *Economic Anthropology - Readings in Theory and Analysis*, LeClair, E. & Schneider, H. (eds.) (see item 352). Chapter 1, pp. 17–39.
31. Malinowski, Bronislaw (1968) '*Kula*: the circulating exchange of valuables in the archipelagoes of Eastern New Guinea', in *Peoples and Cultures in the Pacific*, Vayda, A.P. (ed.). New York.
32. Malinowski, Bronislaw (1968) 'In Tewara & Sanaroa: Mythology of the Kula', excerpt from *Argonauts*, in *Studies in Mythology*, Georges, R.A. (ed.). Homewood, Ill.
33. Malinowski, Bronislaw (1970) 1921 article reprinted in *Cultures of the Pacific*, Harding, T.G. & Wallace, B.J. (eds.) (see item 274).
34. Malinowski, Bronislaw (1973) *Magie, Wissenschaft und Religion, und andere Schriften.* Übersetzung von Eva Krafft-Bassermann. Reihe 'Conditio Humana', S. Fischer-Verlag, Frankfurt a.M.
35. Malinowski, Bronislaw (1973) *Gli Argonauti del Pacifico occidentale.* Newton Compton, Rome.
36. Malinowski, Bronislaw (1974) *Les jardins de corail.* (Trad. de l'anglais par P. Clingnart.) François Maspero, Paris.
37. Malinowski, Bronislaw (1979) *Argonauten des westlichen Pazifik.* Übersetzung von Heinrich Ludwig Herdt. Syndikat-Verlag, Frankfurt a.M.
38. Malinowski, Bronislaw (1979) See Young, Michael (1979) item 554

Government Publications and Reports

The Annual Reports on Papua and New Guinea prepared by the government administrators are of historical and anthropological interest. They contain brief references to the kula in terms of inter-island trade in various goods and comments on native production of items for export such as canoes, pots, carvings, etc. Those of most use for research were published between 1885 and 1928, and have detailed descriptions of particular areas and fascinating accounts of the European responses to native life. Page references are to items which explicitly refer to trade and inter-island contact in the Massim.

39. Macgregor, William (1890) *Annual Report on British New Guinea, 1888-1890*. Government Printer, Brisbane, Australia. Contains reports of the government inspection of some of the Milne Bay Islands. Brief descriptions, observations mainly in terms of geographical features and possible economic exploitation.
40. Macgregor, William (1892) *Annual Report on British New Guinea, 1890-1891*. Government Printer, Brisbane Australia, pp. 66–67, p. xvi, section 28. Information on Panneati which is presented as centre of canoe production. Mentions the use of stone axes as 'the standard of currency for all great transactions' and indicates that steel axe blades are now incorporated in traditional exchanges.
41. Macgregor, William (1894-1896) *Annual Reports on British New Guinea, 1892-1895*. Government Printer, Brisbane, 1892-1893 Report pp. vi-xxv, Appendices, pp. 1-47; 1893-1894 Report pp. xiii-xx, Appendices, sections beginning on pp. 8, 16, 38, 60, 71; 1894-1895 Report pp. xiv-xviii, Appendices, pp. 3, 9, 10, 21, 23. In Appendix G there is specific reference to 'an annual trading trip to Goodenough Island' from Kavatari Island where the chief, Pulitari, interprets an earthquake as a sign of good luck for the voyage. Notes the use of striped axe blades from Murua as a medium of exchange 'all over the East end of the Possession and also in Solomon Islands'. Interesting comments on the use of 'stone tomahawks, armshells,

etc.' in exchange for gardening rights on Samari, mentions also the decline in canoe production. Discusses the use of red sapi-sapi beads and green stone axe blades as 'money', maintaining that 'A string of red native beads, one yard long' is the most valuable item and is the price of a canoe.

42. Macgregor, William (1897) *Annual Report on British New Guinea, 1895–1896*. Government Printer, Brisbane, pp. xi, xiii–xvii. Appendix 5 mentions imports of cooking pots to Dobu Island.

43. Macgregor, William (1898) *Annual Report on British New Guinea, 1897–1898*. Government Printer, Brisbane, Report p. xvii, Appendices pp. 42, 47. Dobuan woman wore a pendant 'ornamented with red shells' (doga?). Also mentions trade between Dobu and the Amphletts.

44. Winter, F.P. (1900) *Annual Report on British New Guinea, 1898–1899*. Government Printer, Brisbane, p. 28, 'Dispatch from visit to the Eastern part of the possession'. Notes the five canoes on Teste Island which were 'made on Utian or Brooker Island and sold for 12 tomahawks'.

45. Anon. (n.d. [?1906] *Annual Report on British New Guinea for year ending 30th June 1905*. Government Printer for the State of Victoria, 1905, pp. 20, 26, 33, 69–72. The Report refers to a government circular, distributed to magistrates, missionaries, etc., enquiring about native trading practices. M.H. Moreton, Resident Magistrate of the S.E. Division, gives a brief summary of a report by Bromilow but states firmly that he thinks there is no trading of any consequence amongst the natives of the Louisiades and that 'The Gumagi mentioned by Mr Bromilow come to the outskirts of the Louisiade Archipelago, Deboyne Island and no further.' He mentions that on Sudest, Rossel Islanders 'come to buy New Guinea pots and dishes and pay in limesticks, armshells, New Guinea money, etc. There is nothing in these visits of any moment . . . ' The Reverend M.K. Gilmour provides 'A Few Notes on the Kiriwina (Trobriand Group) trading expeditions' which give some details.

46. Barton, F.R. (1908) *Annual Report on Papua, 1907*. Government of the Commonwealth of Australia. Contains a report by Dr R.L. Bellamy, 'Notes on the Customs of the Trobriand Islander', which is an important primary source on rank, kinship and totemism in the Trobriands.

47. Murray, J.H.P. (1909) *Papua, Annual Report for 1909*. Government of the Commonwealth of Australia Printer, pp. 103–108, Appendix D. Account of a Patrol on Rossel Island, which gives a brief description of the shell currency there.

48. Murray, J.H.P. (1911) *Papua, Annual Report for 1910*. Government of the Commonwealth of Australia Printer, pp. 84–85. Report on Trobriands mentions men absent 'away on their armshell trading expedition to Murua'.

49. Murray, J.H.P. (1912) *Papua Annual Report, 1912*. Government of the Commonwealth of Australia Printer, p. 112. Mentions that dysentery struck

the D'Entrecasteaux group at the time when the inhabitants were 'indulging in their yearly sail-about'.

50. Murray, J.H.P. (1914) *Papua Annual Report, 1913-1914*. Government of the Commonwealth of Australia Printer, pp. 37-39. Magistrate's Report gives a description of kula. 'The time-honoured custom of sending peace offerings in the shape of *bagi* (sapi-sapi belts and necklets) and *masiwari* (armshells) from island to island is still observed and it speaks well for the character of the people that equivalent values are in all cases returned sooner or later . . .'

51. Murray, J.H.P. (1922) *Papua Annual Report, 1920-1921*. Government of the Commonwealth of Australia Printer, pp. 53-54. Mentions canoe production decline and Mailu traders' 'monopoly' in pots made by women. Contains photographs of canoes and armshell manufacture.

52. Murray, J.H.P. (1923) *Papua Annual Report, 1921-1922*. Government of the Commonwealth of Australia Printer, pp. 26, 28-29. Report on the Anthropology of the S.E. Division. Notes on currency on Rossel and Sudest Islands.

53. Murray, J.H.P. (1925) *Papua Annual Report, 1922-1923*. Government of the Commonwealth of Australia Printer, p. 21. Description of Misima and note on Panaeati Islanders who trade in canoes and pots, keeping other islands in their debt. An interesting source for material on the impact of Europeans on Massim trade.

54. Murray, J.H.P. (1926) *Papua Annual Report, 1923-1924*. Government of the Commonwealth of Australia Printer, p. 22. Report on Woodlark Island by N.G. Linlay notes 'there were several appeals for intercession in connexion with operations under the circular exchange of *masiwari* (armshells) and *bagi* (sapi-sapi armlets, belts and necklets) . . .' which he maintains were formerly 'peace offerings'.

55. Murray, J.H.P. (1927) *Papua Annual Report, 1925-1926*. Government of the Commonwealth of Australia Printer, pp. 42, 44, 47. Report on Resident Magistrate to Eastern Division refers to the Woodlark men on 'walkabout' trading sapi-sapi for armshells and the Trobriand report notes a decline in the value of sapi-sapi in trading.

56. Murray, J.H.P. (1928) *Papua Annual Report, 1927-1928*. Government of the Commonwealth of Australia Printer. Appendix A, 'Indirect Rule in Papua', is a valuable source for understanding contemporary ideas of the nature of native political structure and development. Contains a brief reference to Malinowski's work.

57. Baldwin, Bernard (1967) Vocabulary of Biga Boyowa, the language of the Trobriand Islands. Compiled 1936-1967. Pacific Manuscripts Bureau Microfilm No. 63. Research School of Pacific Studies, Australian National University. About 300 frames. Valuable semantic data on key kula terms interspersed throughout entries.

58. Fellows, Samuel B. (1973) Papers of Rev. Samuel Benjamin Fellows 1894-

1900. Pacific Manuscripts Bureau Microfilm No. 601. Australian National University. Research School of Pacific Studies. 724 frames. Kula material about chieftainship of 1890s, about use of armshells in peace-making ceremonies, values of trade goods, new European commodities, warfare on Kiriwina. Frames 59-65 and *passim*.

59. Jenness, D. (n.d.) [c.1912] Collection of plates for approximately 400 photographs of the D'Entrecasteaux Islands. Pitt-Rivers Museum, University of Oxford. These plates are filed in the catalogue room, in two drawers. They are of fine quality, still able to be used. They contain photographs of ethnographic and historical importance; many concern the material culture.

60. Records of Government and Missions on the Trobriands (1894-1974) Personal microfilm of selected documents in district administration, land matters, education, health, courts, census, transportation, and Methodist mission. 987 frames. Property of Jerry W. Leach. Kula material covers arguments over broken paths and partnerships, sailing by trawler, indigenous valuables and their monetary values, use of valuables for renting land, opposition of mission to kula. Information on frames 95-99, 213, 224, 329-331, 372, 449, 516-519, 582-583, 692, 780-782, 860, 875.

61. Records of Kiriwina Local Government Council (1966-1974) Personal microfilm of records of introduction of council, advertisers' reports, resolutions, financial reports, and register of assets. 750 frames. Also mimeographed copies (in English) of all Council minutes. Personal property of Jerry W. Leach. Council minutes can be located at Council chambers, at Losuia Sub-district Office, and at Office of Local Government in Port Moresby. Kula material is in the Council Minutes.

62. Records of Trobriand Administration (1890-1941) Files of Correspondence, Station Journals, and Patrol Reports from Outstations. British New Guinea and Papua Government Secretary. Archival file CRS G91. Microfilm No. 39-40. Available at Australian Archives, Canberra, and Archives of Papua New Guinea, Port Moresby. Valuable kula material especially in Patrol Reports. Covers economic values of valuables, kula disputes, European relationship to kula, trade and circulation of commodities, changes in canoe building, changes from canoe to trawler voyaging, kula partners of early chiefs, selling of greenstone axeblades to storekeepers. Methodist opposition to kula.

Historical Material

63. Abel, C.W. (n.d. [1902]) *Savage Life in New Guinea: the Papuan in Many Moods.* London Missionary Society. A popular work, judged unreliable by Malinowski, but with some information on the Southern Massim.

64. Affleck, Donald A. (1971) 'Murua or Woodlark Island: a Study of European-Muruan Contact to 1942'. B.A. Honours Thesis, ANU, Canberra. Fred Damon annotates: 'A study of Woodlark's history from initial contact of about 1812 to World War II. Social change focusing on early missionary activities (1848-56), copra trade (1880s to 1942), gold mining (1890s to 1942), and government action (1888-1942).' Extensive bibliography.

65. Andrew, Rev. J.R. (1940) 'Changes in Papuan Social Life'. Summary of a lecture given to Anthropological Society of South Australia, 28th August, 1939, pp. 277-278. Largely concerned with the effects of whites on native life on Misima. 'Several greenstone implements were exhibited, among which there were some ceremonial hatchets and other tools from Woodlark Island. Voyages were still made in connection with the kula ring and blocks of greenstone were procured in exchange for shells and necklets.'

66. Anon. (1960) 'Special Report: The Kula Today', in *Papuan Times*, Port Moresby, May 6, p. 14.

67. Arensberg, C. (1958) See Polanyi, K. (1958) item 420.

68. Austen, John (1974) See Saville, G. (1974) item 115.

69. Austen, Leo (1936) 'The Trobriand Islands of Papua', in *The Australian Geographer*, Vol. 3, No. 2, November, 1936. Brief history of European administration of the Islands, geographical description, flora and fauna; discussion of future patterns of colonization and agricultural development.

70. Beier, Ulli (1978) See Kasaipwalova, John (1978) item 97.

71. Beier, Ulli (1978) See Kasaipwalova, John (1978) item 98.

72. Beledami, N. (1974) 'Bunama - Feasts at Normanby', in *Oral History*, 2:9, pp. 14-19. Not seen by editor.

73. Berde, Stuart James (1974) 'Melanesians as Methodists'. Ph.D. Thesis, University of Pennsylvania, pp. 59, 83-87, 308-314.
74. Bevan, Theodore F. (1890) *Toil, Travel and Discovery in British New Guinea.* Kegan Paul, Trench, Trubner & Co. Ltd., London. On Louisiades and Teste. Marginal.
75. Billy, T. (1974) 'Festival at Dobu', in *Oral History*, 2:9, pp. 28-32. Not seen by editor.
76. Black, Robert H. (1957) 'Dr. Bellamy of Papua', article in three parts in *The Medical Journal of Australia*, Vol. II, No. 6, Sydney, August 10, 17 and 24, 1957, pp. 189-197, 232-238, 279-284.
77. Bromilow, W.E. (1909) 'Some manners and customs of the Dobuans of S.E. Papua', in *Australasian Association for the Advancement of Science*, 1909, Report No. 12, pp. 470-485. Peripheral and probably incorrect. See 'Dr. Bromilow and the Bwaidoka Wars', Young, M.W. (1977) (item 121).
78. Bromilow, W.E. (1912) 'Dobuan (Papuan) beliefs and folklore', in *Australasian Association for the Advancement of Science*, 1911, Report No. 12, (1912), pp. 413-426. Marginal and probably incorrect anyhow.
79. Bromilow, W.E. (1914) 'New Guinea', in *A Century in the Pacific 1815-1915*, Vol. 1, Colwell, J. (ed.). Charles Kelly, London. Bromilow's description of the pioneer missions in the area contains a comment on the traders who upset 'the local way of life', p. 544. Mentions kula objects.
80. Bromilow, W.E. (1929) *Twenty Years Among Primitive Papuans*. London, pp. 125-129. Bromilow was a missionary on Dobu. He claims to have been in the kula which he regarded as a mysterious secret order. For a discussion of his competence as an ethnographer see Fortune, R. *Sorcerers of Dobu*, (1932) (item 242), and Young, Michael (1977) (item 121).
81. Burnett, Frank (1911) *Through Polynesia and Papua*. Francis Griffiths, London, p. 172. Photograph of Trading Canoe, p. 189.
82. Cayley-Webster, H. (1898) *Through New Guinea and the Cannibal Countries.* T. Fisher Unwin, London, pp. 258-260. Marginal, some material on the effects of European trade, particularly the introduction of steel axes on Trobriands and Normanby.
83. Curti, P.A. (1892) 'L'Isola Muju, o Woodlark dei Geografi, nel'Oceania'. Memoria letta il 18 Aprile e 16 Maggio 1861, nel 'Academia Fisico-Medico-Statistica da Milano. Estratto dal Vol. XIV del *Politecnico*, Milan. Held in the Australian Collection, ANU, Canberra.
84. The Editor (1960) 'My view of the *Kula* today', in *Post Courier*, Vol. II, No. 3, May 2. Port Moresby, p. 26.
85. Finsch, Otto (1887) 'Abnorme Eberhauer, Pretiosen im Schmuch der Südsee-Völker, in *Mittheilungen der Anthropologischen Gesellschaft in Wien*. Redacteur Franz Heger, XVII. Band, Wien, pp. 152-159. 'Unusually Shaped Boars' Tusks: Valuable Objects in Dress Ornamentation of South

Sea Islanders'. p. 154 refers to shell armbands made of *Conus millepunctatus* which he calls 'tojas'. They can be exchanged for large quantities of
food but more significantly during this period, he indicates that one armshell 8 or 9 cm in diameter was exchangeable for one American axe.

86. Finsch, Otto (1888) *Samoafahrten. Reisen in Kaiser-Wilhelms-Land und
    Englisch-Neu-Guinea in den Jahren 1884 u. 1885*. F. Hirt & Sohn,
    Leipzig.

87. Gostin, Olga, Tomasetti, W. & Young, M.W. (1971) 'Personalities versus Poli-
    cies', in *The Politics of Dependence: Papua New Guinea, 1968,* Epstein,
    A.L., Parker, R.S. & Reay, Marie (eds.) (see item 225). ANU Press, Can-
    berra. Chapter 3. This article is concerned with the modern political situa-
    tion in the kula district (which encompasses islands which do not kula)
    with a comment on the continuation of the kula.

88. Griffin, H.L. (1925) *An Official in British New Guinea*. Cecil Palmer, Lon-
    don, pp. 185-186, 239. Mentions customs associated with kula and chiefs.
    Of marginal significance.

89. Grimshaw, Beatrice (1908) 'The truth about Papua' (a series), in *Sydney
    Morning Herald*, 23 May, p. 13. Daily newspaper, Sydney, Australia. A
    journalist's account of a journey through Papua. The articles on Rossel
    Island and Sudest contain valuable information about native trade with
    Europeans and indicate that a white trader had already 'instituted a small
    mint' producing sapi-sapi.

90. Grimshaw, Beatrice (1910) *The New New Guinea*. Hutchinson & Co., Lon-
    don, pp. 299-315. Material concerning European intervention in native
    trade and perceptions of the kula in 1910. Useful to compare with *The
    Melanesians of British New Guinea,* Seligmann, C.G. (1910) (see item 481).

91. Hail, B. (1957) 'The well dressed man (in the Trobriand Islands)', in *Walk-
    about* (23, 2), pp. 41-44. Hair adornment.

92. Harrington, Richard (1967) 'Magic of the Trobriands', in *The Geographical
    Review,* Vol. XL, No. 5. London, pp. 355-362. A brief piece of popular
    journalism with some photographs.

93. Hastings, Peter (1969) *New Guinea Problems and Prospects*. Cheshire, Mel-
    bourne, pp. 19, 37. Textbook.

94. Hogbin, H. Ian (1946) 'The Trobriand Islands, 1945', letter in *MAN*, Vol.
    XLVI, May-June, 1946. A letter detailing the changes in Trobriand Islands
    following contact with thousands of allied troops stationed there du.ing
    World War II. Notes the continuation of kula and Mitakata's expedition
    to Dobu.

95. Hurley, Captain F. (1924) *Pearls and Savages. Adventures in the Air, on
    Land and Sea - in New Guinea*. G.P. Putnam's Sons, New York, 1924.
    Includes photographs of Mailu Island production of trading canoe ropes
    and pots. Of minor importance.

96. Kasaipwalova, John (1973) "Modernising Melanesian society - why, and for whom?", in *Priorities for Melanesian Development*, May, Ronald J. (ed.). Research School of Pacific Studies of ANU, pp. 451-454.

97. Kasaipwalova, John & Beier, Ulli (translators) (1978) *Yaulabuta - the Passion of Chief Kailaga: an historical poem from the Trobriand Islands*. Institute of Papua New Guinea Studies, Port Moresby. 48 pp. Kiriwinan text is published in John Kasaipwalova's *Yaulabuta, Kolupa, deli Lekolekwa* (see item 99).

98. Kasaipwalova, John and Beier, Ulli (1978) 'Lekolekwa: an historical song from the Trobriand Islands'. Institute of Papua New Guinea Studies, Port Moresby. 34 pp. A loose song cycle from Iwa now popular in the Trobriands. About plantation experiences, police, Samarai, labour recruiting, catching turtles, sailing, and so forth. The kula material includes jokes about intercourse in canoes (pp. 6-7), sinking on a voyage (pp. 8-9), prizes for a beautiful canoe (pp. 12-13), a husband and a wife arguing over preferred transactions (pp. 16-17), magic (pp. 16-17), an unsuccessful kula tryst (pp. 18-19), diverting a famous necklace (pp. 18-19), strategies of transacting (pp. 22-23), reference to the Myth of the Flying Canoe (pp. 24-25), preparations for a voyage (p. 25), competitive sailing (pp. 26-27), exchanging famous shells (pp. 28-29), 'side-stepping' embarrassing transactions (pp. 30-31), hardships of voyages (pp. 32-33). Note: The Kiriwinan text of 'Lekolekwa' has been published in John Kasaipwalova's *Yaulabuta, Kolupa, deli Lekolekwa* (see item 99).

99. Kasaipwalova, John (1978) *Yaulabuta, Kolupa, deli Lekolekwa*. Institute of Papua New Guinea Studies, Port Moresby. Kiriwinan texts accompanying English texts of the same name.

100. Laracy, H.M. (1970) 'Xavier Montrouzier: a Missionary in Melanesia', in *Pacific Island Portraits*, Davidson, J.W. & Scarr, Deryck (eds.). ANU Press, Canberra.

101. Leach, Jerry W. (1973) 'Making the best of Tourism: The Trobriand situation', in *Priorities in Melanesian Development*, May, Ronald J. (ed.). The Research School of Pacific Studies, ANU, pp. 357-361.

102. Leach, Jerry W. (1976) 'The 1972 Elections in the *Kula* Open', in *Prelude to Self-Government: Electoral Politics in Papua New Guinea 1972*, Stone, David (ed.). Research School of Pacific Studies & University of Papua New Guinea, ANU, pp. 469-491. Account of national electorate covering two-thirds of kula ring in 1972. Basic data on kula area populations, economies, and incomes. Shows how kula was used or avoided by four of seven candidates. Explicit kula references pp. 471, 477, 479, 482.

103. Macgregor, Sir William (1897) *British New Guinea: Country and People*. John Murray, London, pp. 10-12, 21, 24, 25, 26, 51, 57-61, 72, 88, 95.

Several brief descriptions of the Massim with references to trade in food
and other items.

104. Mackay, Kenneth (1909) *Across Papua*. Witherby & Co., London, p. 69.
General description of Massim with single reference to lime spatula carving at Kiriwina.

105. Mead, Margaret (1959) 'A *Kula* expedition and the wives they left behind',
in *Ladies Home Journal*, Vol. 2, No. 1, January, pp. 16-18, 30, 35-37.

106. Meek, A.S. (1912) *A Naturalist in Cannibal Land*. T. Fisher Unwin, London,
pp. 49, 53, 57, 66-73. Chapters 3-5 contain observations of native customs
related to valuables. Interprets *beku* ('tomahawk stones'), *mwali* and *bagi*
as a form of currency.

107. Monckton, Captain C.A.W. (1921) *Some Experiences of A New Guinea
Resident Magistrate*. John Lane, The Bodley Head, London. Monckton's
expositions on the natives are rarely coherent or useful as description –
his racism and contempt prevail against clarity. However, he mentions
some interesting historical changes during the period of European contact
and details of trade with whites. See especially pp. 91-93, 289. Includes
photographs.

108. Moresby, John (1876) *Discoveries and Surveys in New Guinea and the
D'Entrecasteaux Islands*. John Murray, London. Relevant chapters, XII-
XVII, contain numerous observations on the islands of the Massim.

109. Murray, J.H.P. (1912) *Papua or British New Guinea*. T. Fisher Unwin,
London, pp. 114-156. Contains many observations of customs relevant to
the kula in the Trobriands, Woodlark, Sudest, Rossel, Panaeati and Goodenough. Information on canoes and trade items, ceremonial distributions
and inter-island trade in food.

110. Nelson, Hank (1976) *Black, White and Gold: Goldmining in Papua New
Guinea 1878-1930*. ANU Press, Canberra, pp. 3-5, 23, 36, 42-52, 70-72.
A major historical study of European intervention in the Massim with an
excellent bibliography. The notes on the sources for each chapter contain
discussion of the nature and value of particular works.

111. Newton, Reverend H. (1914) *In Far New Guinea*. London. Descriptions of
life in Southern Massim.

112. O'Reilly, Patrick (1931) 'Un Missionaire naturaliste: Xavier Montrouzier
(1820-1897)', in *Revue d'Historie des Missions*, VII, March, 1931. Quoted
by Laracy, H.M. (see item 100).

113. Parkinson, R. (1907) *Dreissig Jahre in der Südsee*. Stuttgart. (Thirty years
in the Pacific. Land and people, manners and customs in the Bismarck
Archipelago and in the German Solomon Islands.) Very extensive collection of ethnographic information by a German trader. Covers the whole
island world of German New Guinea. Stresses material culture and 'cus-

toms'. Weak on social organization. Mentions drift voyages from the Massim to southern New Britain, pp. 241-242.

114. Romilly, H.H (1887) *The Western Pacific and New Guinea. Notes on the Natives, Christian and Cannibal, with some account of the Old Labour Trade* John Murray, London, pp. 127-140, 237-238. Contains one of the earliest descriptions of Woodlark Island and the Laughlan group. Notes interdependence of islands for the provision of essential goods but states categorically that by 1886 the activities of a single trader have ensured that 'the age of stone has vanished' in the area and stone axes are mainly ceremonial, 'exhibited on state occasions'.

115. Saville, Gordon & Austen, John (1974) *'King' of Kiriwina. The adventures of Sergeant Saville in the South Seas.* Leo Cooper Ltd., London. Autobiography of World War II patrol officer.

116. Silas, Ellis (1925) 'An Artist on a Tropic Isle', in *The Wide World Magazine*, Vol. 55, pp. 124-132, especially p. 130.

117. Silas, Ellis (1926) *A Primitive Arcadia.* See especially pp. 106, 107, 113, 122, 124, 149, 181, 183, 184, 205, 211, 224.

118. Thomson, Basil (1889) 'New Guinea: Narrative of an Exploring Expedition to the Louisiade and D'Entrecasteaux Islands', in *Proceedings of the Royal Geographical Society*, Vol. XI, pp. 525-542. Of historical interest containing brief descriptions of initial contact and gold prospecting on Sudest, Rossel, Joannet, St. Aignan, Normanby, Fergusson and Goodenough. Botanical, geographical and ethnographical observations on each area.

119. Tomasetti, W. (1971) See Gostin, Olga (1971) item 87.

120. Young, M.W. (1971) See Gostin, Olga (1971) item 87.

121. Young, M.W. (1977) 'Dr. Bromilow and the Bwaidoka Wars', in *Journal of Pacific History*, Vol. 12, pp. 130-153. About the Christianization of Goodenough and the ideology of trade partnerships. Mentions kula in relation to Bromilow's claim to 'belong' to it.

Anthropological Material

122. Aceves, J.B. (1974) *Identity, Survival and Change: Exploring Social/Cultural Anthropology*. General Learning Press, Morristown, New Jersey, pp. 185-6, 118, Textbook. Kula is cited as an example of ritual exchange, 'closely intertwined' with barter but mainly a prestige activity. Brief summary of trade.

123. Anderson, I. (1922) Review of *Argonauts*, in *New York Times Book Review*, October 29, 1922, p. 10.

124. Anon. (1922) Review of *Argonauts*, in *Boston Transcript*, October 28, 1922, p. 5.

125. Anon. (1922) Review of *Argonauts*, in *Booklist*, Vol. 19, December, 1922, p. 80.

126. Anon. (1922) Review of *Argonauts*, in *New York World*, October 22, 1922.

127. Anon. (1922) Review of *Argonauts*, in *Saturday Review*, No. 134. September 2, 1922, p. 353.

128. Anon. (1971) *Anthropology Today*, Del Mar, Research Machines Inc., pp. 6, 206, 390-393. Textbook. Kula presented as an example of non-utilitarian exchange having social and symbolic functions in Trobriands. Also discussed as an example of functional analysis.

129. Arensberg, C. (1958) See Polanyi, Karl (1958) item 420.

130. Armstrong, W.E. (1924) 'Rossel Island Money: A Unique Monetary System', in *The Economic Journal*, Vol. XXXIV, September, 1924, pp. 423-429. Reprinted in *Tribal and Peasant Economies. Readings in Economic Anthropology*, Dalton, G. (ed.) (1967) (see item 206). Of interest comparatively and for theoretical discussion on the nature of primitive money.

131. Armstrong, W.E. (1928) *Rossel Island*. Cambridge. This study concentrates on Rossel Island's uniqueness and isolation from other Massim islands. Rossel produces sapi-sapi beads for export and apparently possesses other valuables which Armstrong suggests have been 'imported'. He includes photographs of Conus armshells, beads, axe heads, lime spatulae and a ceremonial axe. This work is best known for the section on Rossel Island

money which is important for the debate on the kula, both theoretically and for empirical comparison, especially the attempt to establish a definition of the nature of money in primitive society. The use of the two most valuable shells for blood debt and in marriage (pp. 66–67) and their control by high ranking men suggests that these items share some of the functions of kula objects and are not really in the same category as the other shells. Dalton has criticized Armstrong's interpretation (see item 205) but much earlier Einzig (1949) (see item 220) had made similar points about the inadequacies of Armstrong's data and his failure to establish that *ndap* and *nko* were ever a generalized medium of exchange.

132. Austen, Leo (1938/1939) 'The Seasonal Gardening Calendar of Kiriwina, Trobriand Islands', in *Oceania*, 9, pp. 237–253.
133. Austen, Leo (1940) 'Botabalu: A Trobriand Chieftainness', in *Mankind*, Vol. 2, No. 8, May, 1940. This is a story about a woman chief of the Tabalu subclan. It is largely concerned with conveying ideas about magic and chiefly power. No mention of kula, trade or canoe magic. Marginal.
134. Austen, Leo (1945) 'Nature Handicrafts in the Trobriand Islands', in *Mankind*, Vol. 3, No. 7, April, 1945. Originally written in 1935 – not specifically dealing with kula, but gives details of manufacture of items relevant to kula.
135. Austen, Leo (1945) 'Cultural Changes in Kiriwina', in *Oceania*, Vol. 16, No. 1, September, pp. 15–60. Summary account of the kula at pp. 25–27. The essay as a whole is a useful, general survey which puts Malinowski's various accounts together in one piece.
136. Austen, Leo (1950) 'A Note on Dr. Leach's "Primitive Calendars" ', 'in *Oceania*, Vol. XX, pp. 333–335. Marginal.
137. Baal, J. van (1975) *Reciprocity and the Position of Women*. Van Gorcum, Assen, Amsterdam. This book contains three essays, the first of which examines the problem of reciprocity and exchange theory in terms of trade, criminal and civil law and gift exchange. Comparison of idea of reciprocity in Malinowski, Mauss, Lévi-Strauss and Sahlins.
138. Badcock, C.R. (1975) *Lévi-Strauss – Structuralism and Sociological Theory*. Hutchinson, London, p. 30. Textbook. Kula discussed in relation to Mauss' theory of reciprocity and reference to the structuralist implications of a norm of reciprocity.
139. Bailey, F.G. (ed.) (1971) *Gifts and Poison – The Politics of Reputation*. Basil Blackwell, Oxford, p. 129. Very brief reference to kula in discussing the obligations to *balance* gifts.
140. Balandier, Georges (1972) *Political Anthropology*. Penguin Books, Harmondsworth, pp. 34, 71. Textbook. Translated from French: *Anthropologie politique*. Presses Universitaires de France, 1967. Political significance of kula.

141. Ballantyne, A. & Jenness, D. (1920, 1926/1929, 1938) See Jenness, D. (1920, 1926/1929, 1938) (items 313–314).
142. Baric, Lorraine (1965) 'Some aspects of credit, saving and investment in a 'non-monetary' economy (Rossell Island)', in *Capital, Saving and Credit in Peasant Societies*, Firth R. & Yamey, B. (eds.) Allen & Unwin, London. Relevant to the discussion on primitive money and spheres of exchange.
143. Barnouw, Victor (1975) *Ethnology – An Introduction to Anthropology*, Vol. II. The Dorsey Press, Illinois, pp. 109–111. Textbook. Brief Summary of Malinowski, stress placed on the ceremonial and integrative function of exchange. Republished – 3rd edition, 1978 – same material, book separate, pp. 77–80, kula.
144. Barth, Frederik (1966) *Modes of Social Organization*. Royal Anthropological Institute Occasional Paper No. 23. The University Press, Glasgow, p. 17. Marginal. Draws analogy between the separate spheres of *exchange* in Trobriand society and different spheres of human relationships – e.g. sexual and political 'spheres'.
145. Barton, F.R. (1910) 'The Annual Trading Expedition to the Papuan Gulf', Chapter VII in *The Melanesians of British New Guinea*, Seligmann, C.G. (ed.) (see item 481).
146. Barton, F.R. (1922) Review of B. Malinowski, *Argonauts of the Western Pacific*, in *MAN*, 1922, Article 110, Vol. XXII, December, pp. 189–190.
146a. Battaglia, Debora (1982) 'Syndromes of Ceremonial Exchange in the Eastern Calvados: the view from Sabarl Island', in *The Kula: New Perspectives on Massim Exchange*, Leach, E.R. & Leach, J.W. (eds.) (see item 344).
147. Beals, Ralph L. & Hoijer, Harry (1953) *An Introduction to Anthropology*. Macmillan Co., New York, pp. 369–371, 427–430. Textbook. Example of trade partnerships, found in societies with true division of labour and exchangeable surpluses. Brief description of shell routes. Despite ritual elaboration, it 'is clear that the kula ring functions mainly as a vehicle for trade' (p. 371). Trade after kula transactions. Whole thing seen as 'cumbersome' but it does eventually get the job done.
148. Bell, F.L.S. (1950) 'Travel and Communication in Tanga', in *Oceania*, Vol. XXI, No. 2. No direct mention of kula but description of almost exactly the same institution of exchange of valuables (including armshells) between given islands off the coast of New Ireland.
149. Belshaw, Cyril Shirley (1952) 'Port Moresby Canoe Traders', in *Oceania*, Vol. XXIII, No. 1, September, pp. 26–39. Deals with trade in food. Of no direct relevance to kula as refers to very limited area of Papua, but of interest comparatively.
150. Belshaw, Cyril Shirley (1955) 'In Search of Wealth – A Study of Emergence of Commercial Operations in the Melanesian Society of Southeastern Papua', in *Memoirs of the American Anthropological Association*, Vol. 57, No. 1,

Part 2, Memoir No. 80, February, 1955, Chapter 4, especially pp. 21-30.
This short section includes clear and precise data on exchange in the
Massim. Some interesting details on the production of valuables by elderly
people, 'the products of their leisurely skilled labour', armshells as part of
marriage payment and 'the ceremonial wealth of the two families tied
together to symbolize unity'. The discussion of the *kune* suggests that
there is no distinction between trade partnerships for ceremonial exchange
and those for commerce. Useful maps of trade routes and details based on
fieldwork in early 1950s.

151. Belshaw, Cyril Shirley (1965) *Traditional Exchange and Modern Markets*.
Prentice-Hall Inc., Englewood Cliffs, N.J. Textbook. Chapter 2 'Gift
Exchange and Reciprocity', contains an exposition of the kula.

152. Benedict, Ruth (1935) *Patterns of Culture*. George Routledge & Sons,
pp. 111-115. Textbook. Discussion of Dobuan kula based on Fortune
(1932) and Malinowski. Errors about sources of shells (in an attempt to
explain the directions of the shell valuables). The use of the kula material
is as a demonstration of specific cultural traits on Dobu.

153. Berde, Stuart (1973) 'Contemporary Notes on Rossel Island Valuables',
in *The Journal of the Polynesian Society*, Vol. 82, No. 2, 1973, pp. 188-
205. A discussion of Rossel Island money based on fieldwork in 1971.
Marginally relevant in terms of comparison of 'valuable' exchange.

154. Berde, Stuart (1975) 'Melanesian Distributive Justice', in *Reviews in
Anthropology*, November, 1975, pp. 489-496. Review article of Ekeh
(1974) (item 221) and Schwimmer, E., *Exchange in the Social Structure
of the Orakaiva* (1974) with a discussion of trade partnerships.

155. Berde, Stuart (n.d.) 'Missionizing a Melanesian Society: Religious Syncre-
tism and Exchange on Panaeati Island'. Unpublished paper.

156. Berde, Stuart (1978) 'Melanesian Traders Face-to-Face'. Unpublished Kula
Conference paper. An examination of the mechanics of, and linguistic
modes of enforcing, social obligations of reciprocity. The models are
those of individual Panaeati traders.

157. Berde, Stuart (1979) 'The impact of colonialism on the economy of
Panaeati', in *The Kula: New Perspectives on Massim Exchange*, Leach,
E.R. & Leach, J.W. (eds.) (see item 344). An examination of changes in
subsistence agriculture and canoe production after pacification and the
establishment of the mission. Illustrates the ways in which Christian
values have been incorporated in kula activities and traces an increase
in ceremonialism and the ritual distribution of food. Detailed comparison
of kula exchanges since colonization.

158. Besseignet, P. (1957) 'Essai sur une récherche des principes d'ethnologie
économique'. Thesis, University of Paris. Thesis dealing with Mauss within
an economistic Marxist framework. Interesting attempts to clarify concepts of 'gift' and 'exchange'.

159. Birket-Smith, Kaj (1965) *The Paths of Culture*, translated from the Danish by Karin Fennow. University of Wisconsin Press, Madison, Wis., p. 166. Textbook. [This is a translation of *Kulturens Veja*, two volumes, 1940 and 1942.] A misleading description of the kula trade, based on Malinowski. He presents the kula items as personal ornaments, *mwali* worn by men, *soulava* by women and accounts for their circulation in terms of 'public opinion' being opposed to their possession for 'any great length of time'.

160. Blau, Peter M. (1967) *Exchange and Power in Social Life*. John Wiley & Sons, New York, pp. 89, 93, 99, 106, 110-111. The kula is presented as an exchange affirming friendship and establishing superordination over others. As the object of the relationship is trust, delay in reciprocation is functionally necessary as an indicator of the trust. Discusses Mauss and Homans. Stresses non-utility of objects and the etiquette of kula as a reflection of the social roles of giver and receiver.

161. Blau, Peter, M. (1968) 'Interaction: Social Exchange', in *International Encyclopedia of the Social Sciences*, 7, pp. 452-457. A discussion of the concept 'social exchange' showing that interaction outside the economic sphere has important similarities with economic transactions.

162. Boas, Franz (ed.) (1938) *General Anthropology*. D.C. Heath & Co., New York. Chapter VIII - 'The Economic Organization of Primitive Peoples'. Textbook. See Bunzel, R. (1938) item 176.

163. Bock, Philip K. (1974) *Modern Cultural Anthropology. An Introduction*, 2nd edition. Alfred A. Knopf, New York, pp. 131-132. Textbook. Kula is used as an example in explaining the concept of 'function', particularly 'task function'. Bock's position on the kula itself is that it satisfies a psychological need for prestige.

164. Bohannan, Paul & Dalton, G. (eds.) (1962) *Markets in Africa*. Northwestern University Press, Evanston, Ill. 'Introduction', especially pp.3-13. The kula is discussed in the section on 'Societies without Market Places' in relation to their theory of 'multicentric economy'. Kula and *gimwali* each constitute a separate 'transactional sphere' but there is the potential for inter-sphere transactions, i.e. conversion.

165. Bohannan, Paul (1963) *Social Anthropology*. Holt, Rinehart & Winston Inc., New York, p. 236. Textbook. Kula mentioned in the context of the integration of society. Derived entirely from Malinowski but drawing attention to the variety of exchanges within the kula.

166. Bowman, G. (1977) 'Symbolic Incest and Social Intercourse: Kula and Community in Kiriwina', in *Journal of the Anthropological Society of Oxford*, Vol. VIII, No. 3, Michaelmas, 1977, pp. 158-170. Presents the kula as 'both a metaphor and means for the distribution of authority and the gathering of allegiance ...' on Kiriwina. Stresses inter-island kula and relation to ceremonies which focus on tensions between sub-clan and

the inherent problems of political power in a matrilineal society. Proposes that kula be seen as symbolic incest and marriage.

167. Bradfield, Richard Maitland (1973) *A Natural History of Associations. A Study in the Meaning of Community*. Two volumes, Duckworth, London, Chapter 6, pp. 193-242. An examination of 'the *ethos* of Trobriand Society' involving detailed description of ecology and social structure based on Powell and Malinowski. Kula interpreted as a 'surrogate' for war and discussed in relation to 'pokala' in the community.

168. Brain, Robert (1977) *Friends and Lovers. An anthropological look at friendship*. Paladin, St. Albans, pp. 157-164. Presents a discussion of kula partnership in the context of the chapter 'Business Friends'.

169. Brookfield, H.C. (1969) 'Introduction: The Market Place', in *Pacific Market Places*. ANU Press, Canberra, pp. 1-12. Kula mentioned briefly in context of of a survey of pre-contact trading – the lack of a generalized currency or any price mechanisms is discussed as an essential difference between indigenous trade and market systems.

170. Brookfield, H.C. with Hart, D. (1971) *Melanesia: a Geographical Interpretation of an Island World*. Methuen, London, Chapter 13, 'Location Transfer and Trade in "Old Melanesia"', pp. 324-327.

171. Brookfield, Harold (1973) *The Pacific in Transition*. ANU Press, Canberra, pp. 229-248.

172. Brown, Paula (1970) 'Chimbu Transactions', in *MAN*, Vol. 5, No. 1, pp. 99-117. Discusses kula in comparison with other systems of transaction – uses kinship transactions as analogies.

173. Brunton, Ron (1971) 'Cargo Cults and Systems of Exchange in Melanesia', in *Mankind*, Vol. 8, No. 2, December, pp. 115-128. This article argues that there is a discernible correlation between the disruption of native exchange and the rise of cargo cults. He argues that there have been no cults in the Trobriands or the kula ring because it is a fixed exchange system, 'closed off' and including only traditional valuables – not susceptible to inflation or the incorporation of new items.

174. Brunton, Ron (1975) 'Why do the Trobriands have Chiefs?', in *MAN*, Vol. 10, No. 4, December, pp. 544-558. Argues that the key to the Trobriand political system lies in the degree of control certain *data* leaders gained over kula exchange. Discusses the unique qualities of exchange in Kiriwina arguing for a late involvement in kula. Maps are excellent, conflating information from Belshaw, Fortune, Lauer and Malinowski.

175. Buettner-Janusch, J. (1977) See Rossi, I. (1977) item 446.

176. Bunzel, R. (1938) 'The Economic Organization of Primitive Peoples' in *General Anthropology*, Boas, F. (ed.) (see item 162), pp. 350, 365-366, 460-461. Textbook. Shell valuables are seen as symbols of wealth and the *kula* is associated with the desire to possess wealth. Trobriand economy presented as an equilibrium between the desire to possess and the need to

renounce. In terms of Boas' view of culture, Trobriand society is seen as a 'compromise' between Polynesian–Indonesian and Papuan structures. There is a comparison offered between kula and potlatch.

177. Burling, Robbins (1964) 'Maximization Theories and the Study of Economic Anthropology', in *American Anthropologist*, 64, pp. 802–821. Reprinted in *Economic Anthropology – Readings in Theory and Analysis*. LeClair, E. & Schneider, H. (eds.) (see item 352). A formalist critique of substantivist economic anthropology. Brief reference to kula but theoretically a discussion of issues relevant to all primitive trade.

178. Burns, Tom, Cooper, Matthew & Wild, Bradford (1972) 'Melanesian Big Men and the Accumulation of Power', in *Oceania*, Vol. XLIII, 1972–1973, pp. 104–112. Argument about the control of valuables and exchange in respect to political power.

179. Burridge, K.O.L. (1975) 'The Melanesian Manager', in *Studies in Social Anthropology*, Beattie, J.H.M. & Lienhardt, R.G. (eds.). O.U.P., Oxford, pp. 89–94. Prestige and Exchange. A general discussion of prestige and ceremonial exchange in Melanesia.

180. Campbell, Shirley (1979) *'Kula* in Vakuta: the mechanics of *Keda'*, in *The Kula: New Perspectives on Massim Exchange*, Leach, E.R. & Leach, J.W. (eds.) (see item 344). An exploration of the complex sequences of most exchanges in the kula showing that far from being the 'very simple affair' noted by Malinowski, the modern Vakutan kula involves a series of complicated transactions and a variety of choices for the partners concerned. A detailed description of the processes of exchange.

181. Campbell, Shirley (1979) 'Attaining rank: a classification of *Kula* shell valuables', in *The Kula: New Perspectives on Massim Exchange*, Leach, E.R. & Leach, J.W. (eds.) (see item 344). Examines the value system applied to shell valuables, demonstrating the hierarchical classification in terms of weight, dimension, colour, age and tactile qualities.

182. Carter, Mary (1971) 'The Kula Trade', in *Australian External Territories*, Vol. II, 2, pp. 21–25. Brief account for non-anthropologists.

183. Cassady, Ralph (1974) *Exchange by Private Treaty*. Univ. of Texas Press, Austin, Tex., pp. 25–26.

184. Chapple, Eliot Dismore & Coon, Carleton Stevens (1947) *Principles of Anthropology*. Jonathan Cape, London, pp. 373–374. Textbook. Descriptions and brief functionalist explanation of kula – only source seems to be Malinowski.

185. Chowning, Ann (1960) 'Canoe-Making Among the Molima of Fergusson Island', in *Expedition*, 3:1. The Bulletin of the University Museum of the University of Pennsylvania, pp. 32–40. A description of a canoe maiden voyage and the associated rituals. Mentions increase in inter-island trade since pacification. Many articles are traded but notably 'clay pots, a stone adze blade, a shell bracelet and the pendants of shell and boar's tusk which

are the badge of a headman'. Much of the trade concerned with mortuary rites. Suggests that trade trips are 'primarily a formal method of maintaining peaceful relations'. Excellent photographs. (N.B. Molima does not kula.)

186. Chowning, Ann (1963) Review of Uberoi, J.P. Singh, *Politics of the Kula Ring*, in *American Anthropologist*, Vol. 65, June, p. 743.

187. Chowning, Ann (1977) *An Introduction to the Peoples and Cultures of Melanesia*, 2nd edition. Cummings, Menlo Park, California, p. 50. Brief comparison of kula to other trading systems. Photograph.

188. Chowning, Ann (1978) 'The Massim as a Culture Area'. Unpublished kula Conference paper. An examination of the culture patterns and similarities between those islands designated 'The Massim' stressing common beliefs, practices and cultural unity.

189. Chowning, Ann (1979) 'Wealth and exchange among the Molima of Fergusson Island', in *The Kula: New Perspectives on Massim Exchange*, Leach, E.R. & Leach, J.W. (eds.) (see item 344). Based on fieldwork during 1957-1958 and 1974-1975. Useful data on types of valuables, their customary uses and modes of acquisition amongst a people south of the *kula*. Valuable material on mortuary exchanges and attempts to get Molima into the kula.

190. Codere, Helen (1968) 'Exchange and Display', in *International Encyclopedia of the Social Sciences*, Vol. 5, pp. 240-241. Brief summary of kula exchange and statement of the anthropological problems associated with discussion about the rationale for kula.

191. Codere, Helen (1968) 'Money-Exchange Systems and a Theory of Money', in *MAN*, n.s.3, 1968, pp. 557-577. Discusses the concept of money as 'symbol of goods' and the symbolism of the kula. A substantivist view of money, refers also to Rossel Island's use of 'value without numbers'.

192. Cohen, Percy S. (1967) 'Economic Analysis and Economic Man: Some Comments on a Controversy', in *Themes in Economic Anthropology*, Firth, Raymond (ed.) (see item 237). Tavistock Publications, London, p. 92. Textbook. Discusses Malinowski's conceptions about *Homo economicus* as a Western construction and Firth's critique of this position which emphasizes psychological motives.

193. Collins, J.J. (1975) *Anthropology: Culture, Society and Evolution*. Prentice Hall, Englewood Cliffs, N.J., p. 273. Textbook. Kula ring given as an example of 'ceremonial barter with deferred payments' in section on economics.

194. Colson, Elizabeth (1975) *Tradition and Contract. The Problem of Order*, L.H. Morgan Lectures, 1974. Heinemann, London, pp. 45-47. Brief reference to Malinowski's theory of reciprocity.

195. Coon, C.S. (1947) See Chapple, E.D. (1947) item 184.

196. Cooper, M. (1972) See Burns, T. (1972) item 178.
197. Coppenhauer, Dorian (1977) See Rossi, Ino (1977) item 444.
198. Couper, Alastair (1973) 'Islanders at Sea: Change, and the Maritime Economies of the Pacific', in *The Pacific in Transition*, Brookfield, Harold (ed.) (see item 171). ANU Press, Canberra, pp. 230, 232.
199. Cranstone, B.A.L. (1961) *Melanesia: A Short Ethnography*. British Museum, London. Kula, pp. 23–24. Description of kula focussing mainly on the objects exchanged. Shows photograph of soulava necklace from Teste Island with helmet-shell ornament. Mention of problem of money, trade in pottery, and equipment for betel nut chewing.
200. Crosby, Eleanor (1976) 'Sago in Melanesia', in *Archaeology and Physical Anthropology in Oceania*, Vol. XI, No. 2, pp. 138-155, 145-146, 160. About distribution and making of sago with special attention to tool types.
201. Dalton, George (1961) 'Economic Theory and Primitive Society', in *American Anthropologist*, Vol. 63, No. 1, pp. 143-166. Reprinted in *Economic Anthropology – Readings in Theory and Analysis*, LeClair, E. & Schneider, H. (eds.), Chapter 9 (see item 352).
202. Dalton, George (1962) See Bohannan, Paul (1962) item 164.
203. Dalton, George (1964) 'Economic Theory and Primitive Society', in *Cultural and Social Anthropology*, Hammond, P. (ed.). Textbook. Reprint of *American Anthropologist*, Vol. 63 article (see item 201).
204. Dalton, George (1965) 'Primitive, Archaic, and Modern Economies: Karl Polanyi's Contribution to Economic Anthropology and Comparative Economy', in *Essays in Economic Anthropology*, Helm, J. (ed.). Proceedings of the 1965 Annual Spring Meeting of the American Ethnological Society. Refers briefly to the Trobriands in a general discussion of Polanyi's work, as an example to compare with other societies, their use and division of natural resources.
205. Dalton, George (1965) 'Primitive Money', in *American Anthropologist*, Vol. 67, 1965, pp. 44-65. Reprinted in *Tribal and Peasant Economies. Readings in Economic Anthropology*, Dalton, G. (ed.) (1967) (see item 206). The Natural History Press, N.Y., 1967. A critique of writings on primitive money from a substantivist position. Argues that the terminological confusion between 'special-purpose money' and generalized medium of exchange results in unnecessary obfuscations in literature on exchange of items such as kula shell valuables. Contains a major critique of Armstrong's 'Rossel Island Money' which results in an interpretation of the two top 'denominations' in Armstrong's study looking much more like the shells, boar's tusks, axe blades, etc., of the kula.
206. Dalton, George (ed.) (1967) *Tribal and Peasant Economies. Readings in Economic Anthropology*. The Natural History Press, N.Y., pp. 171-223. Contains two selections from Malinowski's kula writings, 1920 *MAN* article

and Chapter VI of *Argonauts*. Also Armstrong, W.E. (1924) and Dalton, G. (1965) (see items 130, 205).

207. Dalton, George (1971) 'Traditional, tribal and peasant economies: an introductory survey of economic anthropology', in C.B. McCaleb, *Modules in Anthropology*. Addison-Wesley, Reading, Mass. Not seen by editor.

208. Dalton, George (1974) 'Ink-Letting Rites Amongst the Plateau Literati'. Unpublished paper held in Haddon Library, Cambridge. Yet another defence of substantivism – uses kula as an example on a couple of occasions.

209. Dalton, George (n.d.) 'Karl Polanyi's Analysis of Long-Distance Trade and his Wider Paradigm'. Unpublished paper held in Haddon Library, Cambridge, pp. 47–49. This is a useful article, in many ways a 'history of economic anthropology'; and a defence of Polanyi's substantivism. The section on primitive and special purpose money involves a discussion of kula but it is constantly used as an example of a stateless society's economy.

210. Dalton, George (1977) 'Aboriginal Economies in Stateless Societies', in *Exchange Systems in Prehistory*, Earle, Timothy K. & Ericson, Jonathan E. (eds.) (see item 550). Academic Press, London, pp. 191–212. 'This paper constructs [a model of aboriginal economies in stateless societies that employed ceremonial exchanges] emphasizing the importance of relations of alliance and hostility and the special role of primitive valuables in political transactions in stateless societies.' The article focusses on (a) the nature of primitive money debate, (b) kula and political alliance argument (develops some of Uberoi's points) – substitute for warfare, etc., (c) presents some new ideas on the concept of a 'primitive valuable' and the nature of ceremonial exchange.

211. Dalton, George (1978) 'The Impact of Colonization on Aboriginal Economies in Stateless Societies', in *Research in Economic Anthropology*, Dalton, G. (ed.). Jai Press, Greenwich, Conn. Not seen by editor.

212. Damon, F.H. (1978) 'Modes of Production and the Circulation of Value on the Other Side of the Kula Ring'. Unpublished Ph.D. thesis, Princeton University. 'Two modes of production are isolated and discussed. One is called *KULA*, the other is called garden.' This thesis focusses on the social and economic relations structured around the institutions of kula exchange and the production of food. Special attention is given to the concept of *value* on Woodlark as it emerges in exchanges which have an elaborated symbolic significance.

213. Damon, F.H. (1976) 'On Individuals: Spatial and Temporal Aspects of the *Kula*'. Unpublished. On *Kula* from the perspective of Woodlark Island.

214. Damon, F.H. (1979) 'What Moves the *Kula*: opening and closing gifts on Woodlark Island', in *The Kula: New Perspectives on Massim Exchange*,

Leach, E.R. & Leach, J.W. (eds.) (see item 344). An analysis of the meanings of opening and closing kula gifts showing the underlying necessity
for expansion in a system which is concerned with preserving equity at one
level but is essentially a competitive enterprise.

215. De Waal Malefijt, A. (1968) *Religion and Culture.* Macmillan, London Kula
pp. 90, 224, 320-321. Textbook. Mentions that magic is linked with 'the
organization and systematization of economic effort' in the kula. Brief
summary of kula with map. Emphasis on 'the religious framework' of
exchange as a reinforcement of social relations.

216. Dillon, Wilton Sterling (1961) 'Giving, Receiving and Repaying'. Unpublished Ph.D. Thesis, Columbia University.

217. Dupré, Georges & Rey, Pierre-Philippe (1968) 'Réflexions sur la pertinence
d'une théorie de l'histoire des échanges., in *Cahiers Internationaux de
Sociologie*, Vol. 46, Jan-June 1968.

218. Dupré, Georges & Rey, Pierre-Philippe (1973) *Economy and Society*, Vol.
2, No. 2, 1973, p. 149. Translated from French: 'Reflections on the
pertinence of a theory of the history of exchange'. Very brief mention of
kula necklaces as 'elite goods', imperishable and non-consumable.

219. Duvignaud, J. (1973) *Le Langage perdu. Essai sur la différence anthropo-
logique*. P.U.F., Paris. Contains one chapter on Malinowski.

220. Einzig, Paul (1949) *Primitive Money*. Eyre & Spottiswoode Ltd., London,
p. 79, 82. Chapter 13 'Shell and Yam Currencies of the Trobriand Islands'.
Maintains that kula valuables constitute 'special purpose' currency. Suggests
that Malinowski's peculiar bias in economics prevented him from seeing
'. . . that in Trobriand, no less than in many other Melanesian communities
there is a monetary system consisting of several types of currencies, each
one with a limited use'.

221. Ekeh, Peter P. (1974) *Social Exchange Theory: The Two Traditions*. Heinemann Educational Books Ltd., London, pp. 24-30, 30-33, 60n. Argues
against an economistic view of the kula. Maintains that the kula validates
existing social relations rather than altering them and ensures social integration at both personal and societal levels because exchange flow is both
direct and circular. Discusses Mauss' use of the kula as an example of collec-
tivist morality and predicts on the basis of the morality of the kula that the
Trobriands would be more concerned with 'duties' than 'rights' in modern
government.

222. Elkin, A.P. (1953) *Social Anthropology in Melanesia.* O.U.P., Melbourne,
pp. 55-60. Textbook. Mainly presenting an overview of ethnographic data.
Contains a good bibliography of Massim material. Mentions that kula
unites the island groups.

223. Ember, Carol R. & Ember, Melvin (1973) *Anthropology*. Appleton-Century-
Crofts, New York, pp. 286-288. Kula fosters pragmatic utilitarian trade.

Brief discussion of shell routes. 'By the time the visitors leave, they have accomplished a year's trading without seeming to' (p. 287). Kula also keeps tradition of the islands alive. Kula permits wide ownership of valuables.

224. Ember, Carol R. & Ember, Melvin (1977) *Cultural Anthropology*. Prentice Hall Inc., Englewood Cloffs, N.J., pp. 111-112. Brief description of kula.

225. Epstein, A.L., Parker, R.S. & Reay, M. (1971) *The Politics of Dependence: Papua New Guinea, 1968*. ANU Press, Canberra. See author entries Gostin, O., Tomasetti, W. & Young, M.W. (items 87, 119, 120). Begins with a description of the kula district (which includes non-kula islands!) and refers to the continued existence of kula trading throughout the period of colonization and to the present day. Provides a good outline of current political structure in relation to central government.

226. Farrell, Bryan H. (1972) 'The Alien and the Land of Oceania', in *Man in the Pacific Islands. Essays on Geographical Change in the Pacific Islands*, Ward, R.G. (ed.). Clarendon Press, Oxford, p. 37. Discussing the precarious nature of food production he refers to barter attached to kula trade as 'protection against famine or shortages'.

227. Fathauer, George H. (1961) 'Trobriand', in *Matrilineal Kinship*, Schneider, D.M. & Gough, K. (eds.) University of California Press, Chapter 4, pp. 234-269. Textbook. Marginal. Mentions that men of high rank support craftsmen of valuables and that marriages might be negotiated in terms of the mutual advantages of a person from a shell-producing area marrying a person from a good gardening area.

228. Fink, Ruth A. (1964) 'Fieldnotes and Records of Political Meetings of 1964 National Elections in Ea'ala-Losuia Open Electorate'. Held by Ruth (Fink) Latukfu, Department of Anthropology and Sociology, University of Papua New Guinea and by Jerry W. Leach.

229. Fink, Ruth A. (1965) 'The Esa'ala-Losuia Open Electorate', in *The Papua-New Guinea Elections*, Bettison, David G., Hughes, Colin A. & van der Veur, Paul W. (eds.). ANU Press, Canberra, 1965, pp. 284-298.

230. Firth, Raymond (1929) 'Currency, primitive', in *Encyclopaedia Britannica*, 14th edition, Vol. 6, pp. 880-881. Mentions strings of red shell beads constituting a store of wealth, but having limited use as 'currency'. States that Pacific does not have genuine 'money', cf. Africa.

231. Firth, Raymond (1929) 'Trade, primitive', in *Encyclopaedia Britannica*, 14th edition, Vol. 22, pp. 345-346. Kula mentioned as a form of ceremonial exchange similar to N.W. Australian system – notes the institutions of trade partnership and the native distinction between kula and barter.

232. Firth, Raymond (1938) *Human Types*. Nelson, London, pp. 88, 93. Revised edition 1975. Sphere Books, London, pp. 83, 84, 87-93.

Chapter III, 'Work & Wealth of Primitive Communities'. This brief mention raises the issues of value ('In a sense the exchange itself is the thing of value, and not the object', p. 89) and the nature of money – kula items excluded from this category because of specific nature of exchange.

233. Firth Raymond (1952) 'Notes on the Social Structure of Some South-Eastern New Guinea Communities', Part I, Mailu, in *MAN*, Vol. 5, pp. 65-67. Photograph of man displaying mwali and mention of the use of armshells in ceremonial exchange (bridewealth) and in purchasing canoes.

234. Firth, Raymond (1957) 'The Place of Malinowski in the History of Economic Anthropology', in *Man and Culture*, Firth, R. (ed.) (see item 235), pp. 209-228. This essay, whilst assessing Malinowski's theoretical contributions generally, deals specifically and critically with his interpretation of kula as an economic institution.

235. Firth, Raymond (ed.) (1957) *Man and Culture*. Routledge & Kegan Paul, London. Textbook. This collection of essays includes much that is crucial, on a critical level, for an understanding of Malinowski's presentation and interpretation of the kula. Firth's introduction and essay are the only contributions which deal specifically and explicitly with the kula. (See Kaberry, P. (1957) item 318, Leach, Edmund R. (1957) item 342, Nadel, S.F. (1957) item 397, Piddington, Ralph (1957) item 415.)

236. Firth, Raymond (ed.) (1967). *Themes in Economic Anthropology*, A.S.A.6. Tavistock Publications, London. Textbook.

237. Firth, Raymond (1967) 'Themes in Economic Anthropology: A General Comment', in *Themes in Economic Anthropology*, A.S.A.6. Tavistock Publications, London. This essay discusses the relationship between economic theory and anthropological insights into motives behind economic activity – especially those of social or 'moral rule or ritual proscription'. The section on 'The Economics of the Gift', mainly concerned with Mauss' 'The Gift' and with Mauss' and Malinowski's material on the social sanctions involved in ceremonial exchange. Stress on the 'non-economic' elements of kula.

238. Firth, Raymond (1975) 'Seligmann's Contributions to Oceanic Anthropology', in *Oceania*, Vol. XLV, No. 4, June, 1975. Notes Seligmann's failure to recognize the *system* although he saw the concrete elements of kula.

239. Firth, Raymond (1979) 'Magnitudes and values in kula exchange', in *The Kula: New Perspectives on Massim Exchange*, Leach, E.R. & Leach, J.W. (eds.) (see item 344). An examination of the value system of the kula in terms of the economic 'weighting' of each transaction drawing out the 'pricemaking mechanism' of a serial transaction.

240. Forde, Daryll, C. (1934) *Habitat, Economy and Society. A Geographical*

Introduction to Ethnology. Methuen & Co., London, p. 204. Textbook. Kula described in general discussion of oceanic trade which serves both economic and social ends.

241. Forge, A. (1972) 'The Golden Fleece', in *MAN*, Vol. 7, No. 4, December.
242. Fortune, Reo F. (1932) *Sorcerers of Dobu*. Routledge & Kegan Paul, London, pp. 18, 85, 98, 131, 152, 169, 189, 193-194, 198, 200-237, 262, 277. This is the other classic ethnography of the Massim and a major source of comparison with the *Argonauts*. Fortune's study is most often used to demonstrate the underlying utilitarian aspects of kula exchange and as a source for non-Trobriand views of kula. His material deals briefly with the introduction of valuables into the rings, their commodity status and other uses in exchanges for bridewealth, mortuary payments and payments for services. Although some of the Dobuan material contradicts Malinowski's view of the kula, it is important that this work confirms and extends that presented in *Argonauts*, particularly the magic and myths of the kula.
243. Fortune, Reo (1972) *Sorciers de Dobu: anthropologie sociale des insulaires de Dobu dans le Pacifique*. Translated by Nicole Belmont. François Maspero, Paris.
244. Fortune, Reo (1978) 'Memories of the *Kula*'. Unpublished Kula Conference paper. A short discursive paper on the variety of interpretations of Massim trade and social organization offered by observers prior to and including Malinowski.
245. Foy, W. (1913) 'Zur Geschichte der Muschelgeldschnure in der Süsdsee', in *Ethnologica*, 11, 1913, pp. 134-147. (On the history of shell money strings in the Pacific.) Discussion in terms of German culture-historical theory. Concludes that shell money strings are associated with Graebner's 'two class' rather than 'bow' culture layers. Scattered references to S.E. New Guinea.
246. Frankenberg, Ronald (1967) 'Economic Anthropology, One Anthropologist's View', in *Themes in Economic Anthropology*, A.S.A.6, Firth, R.. (ed.) (see item 236), p. 49. Textbook. Of minor importance. A brief reference to Malinowski's being influenced by Bucher in his discussion of the interrelatedness of social and economic relations in the kula.
247. Friedl, John (1976) *Cultural Anthropology*. Harper's College Press, N.Y., pp. 320-322, 360. Textbook summary of the kula, focussing on explanation of Malinowski's methodology which allowed him to move beyond superficial interpretation, extracting deep, functional meaning from apparent irrationality. Map. Also mentions kula with respect to theories of reciprocity.
248. Friedl, J. & Pfeiffer, J.E. (1977) *Anthropology – the Study of People*. Harper's College Press, New York. Kula, pp. 459-461, 486. Textbook. Kula summarized as the exchange of ritually valuable items – basic

reciprocal exchange attached to market exchange which is regulated by supply and demand.

249. Friedman, Jonathan (1975) 'Religion as Economy and Economy as Religion', in *Ethnos*, 1-4, 1975, pp. 46-63. Theoretical article involving comparison of Kachin and various Oceanian exchanges of valuables.

250. Frost, E.L. (1976) See Hoebel, E.A. (1976) item 295.

251. Fusfeld, Daniel B. (1958) 'Economic Theory Misplaced: Livelihood in Primitive Society', in *Trade and Markets in Early Empires*, Polanyi, K., Arensberg, C. & Pearson, H.W. (eds.) (see item 420), pp. 342-355. Refers to the kula as typifying an 'economic' institution only explicable in terms of its 'embeddedness' in other social institutions.

252. Gall, Patricia L. & Saxe, Arthur A. (1977) 'The Ecological Evolution of Culture: the State as Predator in Succession Theory', in *Exchange Systems in Prehistory*, Earle, Timothy K. & Ericson, J.E. (eds.) (see item 550). Academic Press, London, p. 265. Simply refers to Uberoi's conclusions about the link between political power and control over exchange.

253. Gasche, Rodolphe (1972) 'L'échange heliocentrique', in *Marcel Mauss, L'Arc*, Revue Trimestrielle, 48, pp. 70-84. A critical re-examination of Mauss' 'Essai sur le don', focussing on the ambiguous and paradoxical elements in his concept of reciprocity.

254. Gjessing, Gutorm (1956) *Socio-Culture - Interdisciplinary Essays on Society & Culture*. Oslo, p. 141. Textbook. Discusses the theoretical implications of Malinowski's description of the kula in respect to his own theory of 'the socio-cultural system'.

255. Godelier, Maurice (1969) 'La "monnaie de sel" des Baruya de Nouvelle Guinée', in *L'Homme*, 9:2, pp. 5-37. Longer, more descriptive version of article published under same title in 1970.

256. Godelier, Maurice (1970) 'La "monnaie de sel" des Baruya de Nouvelle Guinée, in *Cahiers Vilfredo Pareto*, No. 21. Droz, Genéve. Reprinted in *Horizon, trajets marxistes en anthropologie*, Godelier, Maurice (ed.) (1973) (see item 258).

257. Godelier, Maurice (1972) '"Salt Currency" and the Circulation of Commodities Among the Baruya of New Guinea', in translation item 255, *Studies in Economic Anthropology*, Dalton, G. (ed.) Amer. Anth. Assoc., Washington, 1971, pp. 52-71, esp. 52-55. This article raises issues of a theoretical nature which involve interpretation of the kula. Godelier argues that kula items were never perceived in terms of a market economy and therefore should not be seen as 'special kind of currency'. He says that 'currency' is rarely used and wealth items are not deemed to be capital, but function primarily as media of social exchange. He stresses the double nature of wealth items as commodities and non-commodities.

258. Godelier, Maurice (1973) *Horizons, trajets marxistes en anthropologie*.

François Maspero, Paris. Contains several essays, mostly published previously in French journals – several refer directly to kula.

259. Godelier, Maurice (1977) *Perspectives in Marxist Anthropology*. Cambridge University Press, Cambridge, pp. 15, 38–39, 111–117, 127–128, 202. Discussion of the kula and exchange within the framework of Marxist economics and theories of social relations.

260. Goodfellow, D.M. (1939) *Principles of Economic Sociology*. George Routledge & Son, London. Textbook. Chapter 1. Comparison of kula with African gift exchange – marginal.

261. Gouldner, Alvin W. (1960) 'The Norm of Reciprocity: A Preliminary Statement', in *American Sociological Review*, Vol. 25, 1960, p. 174. Delayed reciprocity is the essence of the 'peace-keeping' element of kula exchange, the state of indebtedness contributing to social stability and integration.

262. Gregory, C. (1979) 'Kula gift exchange and capitalist commodity exchange: a comparison', in *The Kula: New Perspectives on Massim Exchange*, Leach, E.R. & Leach, J.W. (eds.) (see item 344). A comparison of the capitalist mode of exchange with kula within the framework of a Marx–Sraffa theory of money, prices and interest.

263. Groves, M. (1956) See Watson, L. (1956) item 519.

264. Guiart, Jean (1966) 'La Chefferie: Structures et Modèles', in *L'Homme*, Vol. VI, Cahier 1, 1966. Marginal.

265. Guidieri, Remo (1973) 'Il *Kula*: ovvero della truffa. Una reinterpretazione dei pratiche simboliche delle isole Trobriand', in *Rassegna italiana de sociologia*, Anno XIV, No. 4, ottobre–dicembre, pp. 559–593. 'The *Kula*: that is to say Trickery'. Discusses the relationship between courting and kula activities emphasizing the elements of trickery and self-presentation. Draws parallels between war, kula and courtship and the painting of the body is discussed in terms of its structural similarity with canoe ornamentation.

266. Guindi, Fadwa El. (1977) *Religion in Culture*. Wm. C. Brown Co., Dubugne, Iowa, pp. 13–66. Very brief reference, assuming that reader is familiar with *Argonauts*, simply says that magical explanations are offered for failure in kula. Kula ring entry in glossary of terms.

267. Haddon, A.C. (1894) 'Legends from the Woodlarks – British New Guinea', in *Folklore*, V, December, 1894. Translations of Montrouzier and Thomassin on Murua Island. Descriptions of creation myths and myths of fire, sun and moon.

268. Haddon, A.C. (1922) Review of *Argonauts*, in *Nation and Athenaeum*, Vol. 31, August 19, 1922, p. 686.

269. Haddon, A.C. (1922) Review of *Argonauts*, in *Nature*, Vol. 110, October 7, 1922, p. 472.

270. Haddon, A.C. & Hornell, James (1936–1938) *Canoes of Oceania.* Bernice P.

Bishop Museum, Honolulu. Special publications 27–29. Reprinted in 1975 in one volume. A comprehensive study of canoes, particularly with respect to their construction, geographical distribution and historical evolution throughout Oceania. The bibliography and the historical references are extensive and provide the best compilation of early sources yet published.

271. Hage, P. (1977) 'Centrality in the Kula Ring', in *Journal of the Polynesian Society*, 86, pp. 27–36.

272. Hamy, E.T. (1889) 'Etude sur les Papouas de la Mer D'Entrecasteaux', in *Extraits de la Revue d'Ethnographie*, 7 (6), pp. 5–21. Cited in 'Amphlett Islands' pottery trade and the *Kula*', Lauer, P. (1970) (see item 337).

273. Harding, T.G. (1967) *Voyagers of the Vitiaz Strait. A Study of a New Guinea Trade System.* Univ. of Washington Press, Seattle, pp. 21, 59, 123, 244. Several brief references and comparisons with the kula. This study contains much that is of comparative interest, both in analysis of the economic elements and the nature of trade partnerships. Stresses the double nature of trade, as both a peace-making activity and as an economic institution.

274. Harding, Thomas (1970) 'Trading in Northeast New Guinea', in *Cultures of the Pacific*, Harding, T.G. & Wallace, B.J. (eds.). The Free Press, N.Y., pp. 94–111. A detailed analysis of Siassi trading system which depends on comparisons with the kula ring. Stress on complementarity of trade partnerships. Interesting discussion of Fortune's idea of the kula as a 'peace-keeping' institution involving a rejection of the distinction between 'utilitarian' and 'ceremonial' objects.

275. Harding, T.G. (1978) 'Introduction: Major Themes of the Conference', in *Mankind*, 11 (3), 1978, pp. 161–164. In introducing the volume on *Trade and Exchange*, Harding outlines the problems involved in archaeological and anthropological approaches to the study of exchange.

276. Harris, Marvin (1969) *The Rise of Anthropological Theory*. Routledge & Kegan Paul, London, pp. 486–488, 562–567. Textbook. Discussion of Mauss' and Malinowski's theoretical stances and interpretation of kula. Maintains that Malinowski's focus on Trobriand definitions combined with his anti-economic stance produce an analysis both 'irrelevant and obscurantist'.

277. Harris, Marvin (1975) *Culture, People, Nature*. Harper Row, New York, pp. 287–288. Brief discussion of kula.

278. Hart, D. (1971) See Brookfield, H.C. (1971) item 170.

279. Harwood, Frances (1966) 'Structural Co-ordinates of Trobriand Myth', in *Anthropology Tomorrow*, Vol. XI, No. 1, pp. 38–45. Myths examined according to distinctions of type and 'sequence' – associated with *direction* of kula.

280. Harwood, Frances (1976) 'Myth, Memory and the Oral Tradition: Cicero in

the Trobriands', in *American Anthropologist*, Vol. 78, No. 4, December, 1976. Harwood uses Trobriand myths to argue that the locational elements '(1) act as a mnemonic device for the recall of a corpus of myth, (2) as a structural marker dividing corpus into conceptual units, (3) as a means of restricting social change ...' The kula is discussed in terms of the myths attached and as a relatively stable institution.

281. Hatch, Elvin (1973) 'Culture and man's inborn character: Bronislaw Malinowski', in *Theories of Man and Culture*. Columbia University Press, New York, pp. 272-335. A study of Malinowski's theories of human nature, instincts and necessities and the ways these are expressed socially and culturally. The kula is discussed in terms of Malinowski's ideas about its rationale.

282. Haviland, William A. (1974) *Anthropology*. Holt, Rinehart & Winston. New York, p.429. Textbook. Craft specialization in manufacture of valuables.

283. Haviland, William A. (1978) *Cultural Anthropology*, 2nd edition. Holt, Rinehart & Winston, New York, pp. 274-275. Textbook. Discusses kula as a mode to control the potential dangers of 'negative reciprocity' by 'making relations more sociable than they would otherwise be'. Brief discussion of the shell routes. Closes with statement as to the multi-functional nature of kula trade, typical of 'the close interrelationship of cultural factors ... characteristic of non-Western societies'.

284. Hays, H.R. (1958) *From Ape to Angel: An Informal History of Social Anthropology*. Methuen & Co. Ltd., London, pp. 325-326, 394. Textbook. A popular work, surveying anthropology through the perspective of brief biography. The section on Malinowski is both anecdotal and critical, involving a brief discussion of the kula and Malinowski's functionalism – mentions Malinowski's influence in later theories of exchange.

285. Heath, Anthony (1976) *Rational Choice and Social Exchange*. C.U.P., Cambridge, pp. 51-58, 117-138. Heath discusses the extent to which obligations and rights in the kula are rational. He differentiates types of exchange along Malinowski's lines but stresses the elements of rationality in trade with respect to the maintaining of status. Discusses the necessity for a 'social norm of reciprocity' in kula exchange.

286. Heider, Karl G. (1969) 'Visiting Trade Institutions', in *American Anthropologist*, Vol. 71, No. 3, June, pp. 462-471. A brief but quite wide-ranging study of visiting trade as an institution which, by including elements of internal social relations (kin ties), stresses the closeness of trade partnerships. Presents this as a way of analytically conflating utilitarian and symbolic interpretations of the kula. Good bibliography.

287. Heider, Karl G. (n.d.) *Ethnographic Film*. University of Texas Press, Austin, p. 13. Textbook. Discusses Malinowski's reconstruction of a kula voyage as a technique readily transferred to filming.

288. Herskovitz, Melville J. (1940) *The Economic Life of Primitive Peoples.* Alfred A. Knopf, New York, p. 236. Textbook. Role of 'valuables' in kula, relationship to money.

289. Herskovitz, Melville J. (1948) *Man and His Works: The Science of Cultural Anthropology.* Alfred A. Knopf, New York, p. 221. Textbook. Kula shows the integration of culture. Malinowski studied not only the subsistence range of Trobriand patterns of production, but also moved into the realm of their prestige economy.

290. Herskovitz, Melville J. (1955) *Cultural Anthropology.* Alfred A. Knopf, New York, p. 155. Textbook. Kula a system of value as opposed to pragmatic exchange. These two functions (exchange and value) are bound up in a single currency, money, in Western economies but are often separated in non-literate societies.

291. Hiebert, Paul G. (1976) *Cultural Anthropology.* Lippincott, Philadelphia, pp. 304–305. Textbook. Mentioned under heading 'Types of economic systems'. Kula presented as a means of providing 'security in hostile territories', thereby facilitating economic trade. Map.

292. Hoebel, E. Adamson (1949) *Man in the Primitive World. An Introduction to Anthropology.* McGraw-Hill Book Co. Ltd., New York, pp. 348, 351. Textbook. In section on 'Gifts, Trade & Inheritance', kula is mentioned in terms of the trade in specially produced items and the social relationship structured around reciprocal gift giving. Kula is briefly described, with a lengthy quote from Malinowski's *Argonauts.*

293. Hoebel, E. Adamson (1954) 'The Trobriand Islanders: Primitive Law as Seen by Bronislaw Malinowski', in *The Law of Primitive Man.* Harvard University Press, Cambridge, Mass., pp. 177–210. Textbook. Only indirectly relevant.

294. Hoebel, E. Adamson (1958) *Anthropology: The Study of Man.* McGraw-Hill Book Co., New York, p. 349. Textbook, reprinted several times, 4th edition 1972. Map has some errors. Mentioned in relation to 'Economic Organization', and to the inter-connectedness of social institutions 'trade, magic, ceremonial exchange, overseas travel and pleasure-seeking'.

295. Hoebel, E. Adamson & Frost, Everett L. (eds). (1976) *Cultural and Social Anthropology.* McGraw-Hill Book Co., New York, pp. 259–260. Textbook. Section on kula adapted from *Anthropology: The Study of Man*, Hoebel, E.A. (see item 294).

296. Hogbin, H. Ian (1935) 'Trading Expeditions in Northern New Guinea', in *Oceania*, Vol. V, No. 4, June, 1935, pp. 375–407. An examination of Schouten Island's trading, implicitly comparative with Malinowski's *Argonauts.*

297. Hogbin, H. Ian (1947) 'Native Trade Around the Huon Gulf, North Eastern New Guinea', in *Journal of the Polynesian Society,* Vol LVI Marginal. Of comparative significance only.

298. Hogbin, H. Ian & Wedgwood, Camilla H. (1953) 'Local Grouping in Melanesia', in *Oceania*, Vol. XXIII, No. 4, June, 1953, and Vol. XXIV, No. 1, September, 1953. Mention of ceremonial trading as factor in social cohesion. Marginal.

299. Hogbin, H. Ian (1958) *Social Change*. Watts, London, pp. 196-197, 232n. Textbook. Several references to the Trobriands including a summary of H. Powell's material on chiefly power which mentions the chief's decision to kula and a prediction that the Trobriands might be more susceptible to 'nativism' because of their beliefs in magic. Generally useful for data on change due to European influence in the area.

300. Hoijer, Harry (1953) See Beals, Ralph L. (1953), item 147.

301. Holdsworth, David (1972) *Trobriand Islands*. Rigby Limited, Sydney. Thirty-two page picture album. Pictures taken about 1970. Numerous errors in text. Painting a canoe page 14. Picture of a real chama and an imitation plastic necklace (*kuwa*) on page 22. Model Kitavan canoe on page 27. Very unusual armshell (*mwali*) on back cover.

302. Homans, George Caspar (1961) *Social Behaviour, Its Elementary Forms*. Harcourt, Brace & World Inc., N.Y., pp. 316-320. Textbook. Discussion of exchange relationships in primitive societies as an expression of an equal or close social relationship. Refers to Mauss.

303. Hornell, James (1936-1938) See Haddon, A.C. (1936-1938) item 270.

304. Howells, William (1973) *The Pacific Islanders*. Weidenfeld & Nicolson, London, p. 28. Discussing cultural homogeneity, remarks on the ubiquity of competitive display for prestige kula mentioned.

305. Howlett, Diana (1973) *Papua New Guinea: Geography and Change.* Nelson, Melbourne, p. 144. Comment on the decline in commercial trading but the continuation of the kula between the Louisiade, D'Entrecasteaux and Trobriand Islands.

306. Hoyt, Elizabeth E. (1926) *Primitive Trade - Its Psychology and Economics.* Kegan Paul, Trench, Trubner & Co. Ltd., London, pp. 129-130. Brief mention of kula.

307. Hunter, D.E. & Whitten, P. (eds.) (1976) *Encyclopedia of Anthropology*. Harper and Row, New York, pp. 231-232. Textbook. Entry on '*Kula* Ring', attributes the discovery to Malinowski but is otherwise misleading. Suggests that *mwali* are made from 'white cowrie shell' and that kula 'operates in a circle comprising all the items', although the illustrated map shows this to be wrong. Incorrectly states that *gimwali* operates between kula partners. Other trade routes and comment on the persistence of the kula seem correct.

308. Hunter, David E. & Whitten, Phillip (eds.) (1977) *The Study of Cultural Anthropology*. Harper and Row, New York, pp. 165-167. Textbook.

Credits Malinowski with being the major pioneer in development of economic anthropology. Brief discussion of the shell routes. Closes with Harris' comment to effect that the islanders actually deal not only in shells but in utilitarian items as well. Concludes that a modern analyst would 'certainly focus on the latter aspects, seeing the kula as a supportive mechanism'.

309. Irwin, Geoffrey (1979) 'Chieftainship, kula and trade in Massim prehistory', in *The Kula: New Perspectives on Massim Exchange*, Leach, E.R. & Leach, J.W. (eds) (see item 344). A paper in three parts. 'The first describes a spatial analysis of ethnographic data from the Trobriands and advances another theory on the origins of chieftainship. The second part investigates locational factors within the wider kula network, in order to throw light on aspects of its development. The third considers the emergence of the kula within the more general context of the development of trade and economic specialisation in the Massim.'

310. Jansen, Victor J. (1961) *De Trobriand Eilanden: een door ergelyke aristocratie beheerste maatschappij.* Museum voor Land-en Volkenkunde, Rotterdam. Not seen by editor.

311. Jarvie, I.C. (1964) *The Revolution in Ahthropology.* Routledge & Kegan Paul, London, pp. 18, 39, 183. Uses kula to illustrate his argument on the shortcomings of Malinowski's 'positivist functionalism'. He also criticizes Malinowski's misinterpretation of evolutionists. On the apparent irrationality of the kula he suggests that 'functionalism was *generated* by the peculiarities of the kula'.

312. Jenness, D. & Ballantyne, A. (1920) *The Northern D'Entrecasteaux.* Oxford, pp. 34–35. The authors note the recent decline in trade between Goodenough and the Trobriands. Inter-community trade is seen as main factor in establishing political and social integration. No distinction between ceremonial exchange and commercial transactions. Details of items traded between the groups. An important pre-Malinowskian source.

313. Jenness, Diamond & Ballantyne, A. (1926–1929) 'Language, mythology, and songs of Bwaidoga, Goodenough Island, S.E. Papua', in *Journal of the Polynesian Society*, Vols. 35, 36, 37, 38. The kula appears in three of the songs in Vol. 37, pp. 162, 286–287, 289. Vol. 36, Myth No. 15, 'The Two Parrots', translated on pp. 162–164, is a complex myth of origin which refers to kula items, association them with high rank.

314. Jenness, D. & Ballantyne, A. (1938) The articles which appeared over four volumes in the *Journal of the Polynesian Society* (see item 314) printed together as *Memoirs of the Polynesian Society*, No. 8.

316. Jordan, D.K. & Swartz, D.K. (1976) *Anthropology. Perspective on Humanity.* John Wiley & Sons Inc., New York, pp. 395–497. Textbook.

Kula is discussed in chapter on economics referring to ceremonial and utilitarian trade. 'Kula falls somewhere between our models of generalized and balanced reciprocity.' Discusses techniques of exchange. Map.

317. Julius, Charles (1960) 'Malinowski's Trobriand Islands', in *Journal of the Public Service of the Territory of Papua & New Guinea*, Vol. 2. A summary of the kula for the lay reader.

318. Kaberry, Phyllis (1957) 'Malinowski's Contribution to Fieldwork Methods and the Writing of Ethnography', in *Man and Culture*, Firth, R. (ed.) (see item 235), pp. 77, 83–84. The kula is mentioned in the course of discussing Malinowski's fieldwork and the ways in which the structure of an expedition provided the thematic base for his writing-up.

319. Kardiner, Abram (1939) *The Individual and His Society: The Psychodynamics of Primitive Social Organization*. Columbia University Press, New York, pp. 79–82. Textbook. An explanation of functional analysis using Malinowski's Trobriand material. The description is very abridged and actually reads like a collection of non-related observations and as such seems a singularly unsuccessful presentation of the integration of various institutions within a society.

320. Kardiner, Abram & Preble, Edward (1962) *They Studied MAN*. Secker & Warburg, London, pp. 160ff. 'Bronislaw Malinowski, Man of Songs'. This is a biographical sketch which attempts to situate Malinowski in the history of anthropology. It offers some information on the formative influences on his intellectual development, in particular with respect to his theories of functionalism.

321. Keesing, Felix M. (1958) *Cultural Anthropology: The Science of Custom*. Rinehart & Co. Inc., New York, pp. 151–152. Textbook. The section explaining *functionalism* uses Malinowski's examination of the kula to explain his notion of *function* and a 'science of culture '. Emphasis on Malinowski's influence and his use of the concept of 'needs' in providing explanations of social behaviour.

322. Keesing, R.M. & F.M. (1971) *New Perspectives in Cultural Anthropology*. Holt, Rinehart & Winston Inc., New York, pp. 303–305. Textbook. Contains lengthy quote from Malinowski (1925) on the 'rationality' of Trobriand magic as an explanation for the otherwise inexplicable failure on the part of partners to exchange.

323. Keesing, Roger (1976) *Cultural Anthropology*. Holt, Rinehart & Winston Inc., New York, pp. 307–388 On trade and kula in Melanesia, and elsewhere. Textbook. Kula and Trobriand exchange used as examples of 'the sophistication and complexity of systems of redistribution in so-called primitive societies ...' Contains map and drawings of *mwali* and *soulava*. Differentiates between inland and overseas kula. Quotes Malinowski on the actual exchange process with 'initial gift', 'restoration gift', etc. and

Reo, F. Fortune (1932), p. 217, (see item 242) on the strategies of a kula partner. p. 324, 'kula exchange is intimately bound up with the system of social stratification ...' An accurate presentation of Malinowski's material, also contains references to most other work on the kula in major monographs, including Weiner's recent material.

324. Keil, Dana (1977) 'Markets in Melanesia? A Comparison of Traditional Economic Transactions in New Guinea with African Markets', in *Journal of Anthropological Research*, Vol. 33, No. 3, Fall, 1977, pp. 258-276. A critical study, proposing distinctions between ceremonial and utilitarian trade and partnerships, as opposed to markets, to clarify different systems of exchange - of theoretical importance.

325. Kennedy, Raymond (1945) *The Island Peoples of the South Seas and Their Cultures*. American Philosophical Society, Philadelphia, pp. 47, 86. Textbook. Mentions kula as an institution preserving 'the peace of the market place'. Kula items referred to as 'ornaments with magical significance' and Malinowski presented as an economic determinist.

326. Kirk, G.S. (1970) *Myth, Its Meaning and Functions in Ancient and Other Cultures*, Cambridge University Press, Cambridge and University of California Press, Berkeley. Ch. 1, 'Myth, Ritual and Folktale' pp. 20, 39. Presents myth as wish-fulfilment, the underlying meaning of kula myths of regeneration being the identification of the desire for success in ceremonial exchange.

327. Kirsch, A. Thomas (n.d.) See Peacock, J.L. (n.d.) item 409.

328. Kluckhohn, Clyde (1943) 'Bronislaw Malinowski. 1884-1942', in *Journal of American Folklore*, Vol. 56, 1943, pp. 208-219. Marginal.

329. Kottak, Conrad Philip (1974) *Cultural Anthropology*. Random House, New York, pp. 166, 188-189. Textbook. Discusses kula in context of specialized technology, noting that only two Trobriand villages manufactured kula goods and their location was not related to natural occurrence of raw materials. Also notes Malinowski's ideas on magic in respect to the control of weather.

330. Kottak, Phillip (1974) *Anthropology. The Exploration of Human Diversity*. Univ. of Michigan Press, p. 370. Kula mentioned under 'Specialization', noting that on the Trobriands, 'only two of many villages manufactured certain ceremonial items important in a regional exchange network'.

331. Krieger, Herbert William (1943) 'Island Peoples of the Western Pacific: Micronesia and Melanesia', in *War Background Studies*, No. 16. Smithsonian Institute, Washington, p. 52. Kula mentioned under 'Arts & Crafts' as a unique ceremonial exchange. Refers to kula expeditions as *Lakatoi*. Minor.

332. Krzyżanowski, Jan (1931) 'Z zagadnień socjologicznych państwa pierwotnego', in *Przegląd Socjologiczny,* Vol. 1, 1931, pp. 210-263.

333. Kuper, Adam (1973) *Anthropologists and Anthropology: The British School 1922-1972.* Allen Lane, London, pp. 13-50. Contains an account and an evaluation of Malinowski's work, though no particular account of the kula.

334. Labouret, H. (1953) 'L'Échange et le commerce dans les archipels du Pacifique et en Afrique tropicale', in *L'Histoire du commerce*, Livre 1, Tome 3, Paris, Lacour-Gavet, J. (ed.), pp. 9-125. Not seen by editor.

335. Langness, L.L. & Weschler, J.C. (1971) *Melanesia. Readings in a Culture Area.* Chandler Publishing Co., Scranton, Pa., p. 15. Mention in Introduction to Part I – 'Ecology & Economics'. Comparison drawn with Western Highlands of Papua New Guinea.

336. Laracy, Hugh M. (1970) 'Xavier Montrouzier: a missionary in Melanesia', in *Pacific Islands Portraits,* Davidson, J.W. & Scarr, D. (eds.) ANU Press, Canberra, p. 137. Explains Montrouzier's misunderstanding of native Muruan politics. Muruan surplus food production trader with other islands for artefacts – 'pig's teeth, bones of whale and cassowary'.

337. Lauer, Peter K. (1970) 'Amphlett Islands' pottery trade and the kula', in *Mankind*, Vol. 7, No. 3, June, pp. 165-176. In this article Lauer argues that the kula was originally an integral part of inter-island commodity exchange. Pacification and European trade have altered both kula and commerce, so that the kula is now most significant politically and as 'sentimental trade' between rather isolated island communities. Trade routes for pottery, etc. have altered and Lauer argues that archaeological evidence does not support Malinowski's view of the kula as an immutable system and that instead '... the kula appears to be but another trade system ... in the past, the kula seems to have been subjected to major changes in its geographical dimension and ultimate purpose ...'.

338. Lauer, Peter K. (1970) 'Sailing with the Amphlett Islanders', in *Journal of the Polynesian Society*, Vol. 79, No. 4, December, 1970. Contains photographs of canoes. A detailed description of canoes, their sea-worthiness, and the sailing techniques of Amphlett men who are great traders. Reveals the dangers of kula journeys and indicates effects of Europeans and the introduction of new craft.

339. Lauer, Peter K. (1976) 'Field Notes from the D'Entrecasteaux and Trobriand Islands of Papua', *Occasional Papers in Anthropology*, No. 7. University of Queensland. Contains detailed information on the current state of kula trading between islands of the D'Entrecasteaux group and the Trobriands. Copiously illustrated with data on the production of kula items and other Massim technology – canoe-making, pottery, basketry, etc. Archaeological deposits discussed as evidence of inter-island contact. An important section on kula affiliations as perceived by Amphlett Island men and on sea-voyaging in the Massim area.

340. Lawton, R.S. (1968) 'The Class Systems of Kiriwinan Society'. Unpublished

paper prepared for Translators' Institute, Banz (Western Highlands Province), August, 1968. 15 pp. and 5 appendices. Interpretation of aspects of rank, chieftainship, privileges of decore, leadership, and warfare. Lists different kinds of valuables and shows how they are worn.

341. Leach, Edmund R. (1950) 'Primitive Calendars', in *Oceania*, Vol. XX, No. 4, pp. 245-262.

342. Leach, Edmund R. (1957) 'The Epistemological Background to Malinowski's Empiricism', in *Man and Culture*, Firth, R. (ed.) (see item 235), p. 133. The kula only specifically mentioned as an example of Malinowski's empiricist interpretation of its purpose.

343. Leach, Edmund R. (1978) 'The Kula in its Historical Context'. Unpublished Kula Conference paper. A reassessment of the kula in terms of Malinowski's works and other earlier sources arguing particularly that kula items did function as a form of currency.

344. Leach, E.R. & Leach, J.W. (eds.) (1982) *The Kula: New Perspectives on Massim Exchange.* Cambridge University Press.

345. Leach, Jerry W. (1975) 'Ethnographic Companion to *The Kula*'. Unpublished but to be circulated through Royal Anthropological Institute Film Lending Library. Six page paper (unpublished) to accompany S. Szabo *The Kula* 16 mm documentary distributed in Papua New Guinea and in Britain by the RAI Film Lending Library. Paper gives thumbnail sketch of kula and references. Draws attention to strengths and weaknesses of 1967 film. Specially focusses on differences between simultaneous and delayed exchange. Criticizes the 'kula in decline' theme of the film's narration.

346. Leach, Jerry W. (1978) 'The Kabisawali Movement in the Trobriand Islands'. Unpublished Ph.D. Thesis at Cambridge University. 337 pages. Extended discussion of 1972-1977 period in Trobriand politics and why the society divided the way that it did. Kula and leadership pp. 56, 70-71. Local participation in kula films p. 69. How Kabisawali and its opposition competed via kula in 1973 pp. 193-202. Early contact with trade p. 248. Modern occupations and kula pp. 281-284. Changes in other Trobriand ceremonial exchanges pp. 291-294. Changes in chieftainship system pp. 295-297.

347. Leach, Jerry W. (1978) 'Imdeduya: analysis of a kula folktale from Kiriwina'. Unpublished paper from Kula Conference. An interpretation of a folktale undertaken on two levels, as a moral lesson about courtship and marriage and analogously concerned with the obligations entailed in kula exchanges.

348. Leach, Jerry W. (1979) 'Trobriand territorial categories and the problem of who is not in the *Kula*', in *The Kula: New Perspectives on Massim Exchange*, Leach, E.R. & Leach, J.W. (eds.) (see item 344). An exploration of the various categories applied to determine discrete regions on the

Trobriands and a discussion of kula participation in terms of the five decisive factors – topographical separation, coastal–inland orientation, economic conditions, warfare and ranking associated with kula activity.

349. Leach, J.W. (1982) See Leach, E.R. (1982) (see item 344).
350. Lebra, Takie Sugiyama (1975) 'An Alternative Approach to Reciprocity', in *American Anthropologist*, Vol. 77, p. 559. This is a critique of Sahlins' article (1965) on types of reciprocity (see item 451). He attempts to deal with anomalies in Sahlins' model by 'taking into consideration both the positive and negative manifestations of sociability'. Kula mentioned very briefly in an elaboration of 'Triadization' in exchange, in opposition to a dyadic view of reciprocity.
351. LeClair, Edward E. (1962) 'Economic Theory and Economic Anthropology', in *American Anthropologist*, Vol. 64, 1962, pp. 1179ff. Reprinted in *Economic Anthropology – Readings in Theory and Analysis,* LeClair, Edward & Schneider, Harold (eds.) (see item 352). An argument for a theory of primitive economics involving an attack on Dalton's substantivism. LeClair begins by acknowledging Malinowski's influence in the discipline. He suggests that the concept of a 'market' can be applied to the kula.
352. LeClair, Edward & Schneider, Harold (eds.) (1968) *Economic Anthropology – Readings in Theory and Analysis.* Holt, Rinehart and Winston Inc., New York. Textbook. A thematically constructed textbook, a collection of major contributions to economic anthropology. See Malinowski (item 6), LeClair (item 351), Burling (item 177), Dalton (item 201), and Polanyi (item 420). Conclusion by editors makes some comments on interpretation of kula exchange.
353. Lee, Dorothy (1950) 'Codifications of Reality. Lineal and Nonlineal', in *Psychosomatic Medicine*, 12, 1950, pp. 89–97. Reprinted in *Everyman his Way – Readings in Cultural Anthropology,* Dundes, Alan (ed.), Prentice Hall, Englewood Cliffs, N.J., 1968, also reprinted in *Conformity and Conflict*, Spradley, J.P. & McCurdy, David W. (eds.), Little, Brown, Boston, 1974. This article is a philosophical elaboration of Malinowski's argument about the lack of 'historical' awareness in Trobriand culture. Lee argues that the *language* lacks any notion of lineality, progress or cause/effect relationship in time. Kula is referred to as embodying this codification of reality as entirely synchronic.
354. Lee, Dorothy (1954) 'Being and Value in Primitive Society', in *Primitive Heritage. An Anthropological Anthology,* Mead, M. & Calas, N. (eds.) Victor Gollancz Ltd., London, 1954. This article originally appeared in 1949 in *The Journal of Philosophy*, Vol. XLVI, pp. 401–415. An article arguing that language determines the conceptual framework for the systems of time and value in a culture. Stresses the synchronic mode of thought in Trobriand culture.

355. Lee, Dorothy (1940) 'A Primitive System of Values', in *Philosophy of Science*, Vol. VII. Baltimore, pp. 355-378. Makes use of Malinowski's material on Kiriwina to ask where motivations, direction and control are located in Trobriand way of life. Relates linguistic structures to the kula values maintaining that for the Trobriander an act or object is seen as an end in itself. Questions some of Malinowski's translations of metaphor and causal argument.

356. Lee, Dorothy (1959) *Freedom and Culture.* 3 Chapters, pp. 78-120. Malinowski's work constitutes the only source for these interpretations of Trobriand values in terms of the linguistic structure.

357. Lenoir, Raymond (1924) 'Les expéditions maritimes, institution sociale en Mélanésie occidentale', in *L'Anthropologie*, Vol. 34, Paris. Essentially a review-article discussion of *Argonauts*, giving a good résumé of Malinowski's account. The original element is that Lenoir suggests that *uvakalu* explains the relationship of kula. To some extent Malinowski later accepted this view when he said that kula was 'a surrogate for war'.

358. Lepowsky, Maria (1979) 'Sudest Island and the Louisiade Archipelago in Massim exchange', in *The Kula: New Perspectives on Massim Exchange*, Leach, E.R. & Leach, J.W. (eds.) (see item 344). Based on Sudest Island fieldwork 1978-1979. Discusses the kula in terms of terminology, flow, uses and values of shell necklaces, greenstone axe blades and other valuables in the Louisiade. Contains information on other trade.

359. Lévi-Strauss, Claude (1949) *Les Structures Elémentaires de la Parenté.* Presses Universitaires de France, Paris. See notes for English translation.

360. Lévi-Strauss, Claude (1950) 'Introduction à l'oeuvre de Marcel Mauss', in *Sociologie et Anthropologie*, Mauss, M. (ed.). Presses Universitaires de France, Paris.

361. Lévi-Strauss, Claude (1958) *Anthropologie Structurale*. Librairie Plon, Paris. See notes for English translation.

362. Lévi-Strauss, Claude (1962) *La Pensée Sauvage.* Librairie Plon, Paris.

363. Lévi-Strauss, Claude (1966) *The Savage Mind.* Weidenfeld & Nicolson, London.

364. Lévi-Strauss, Claude (1968) *Structural Anthropology*. Translated by Claire Jacobson and Brooke Grundfest Schoepf. Allen Lane, London, pp. 297-338. First published 1963, Basic Books, N.Y. Two brief references to kula as examples of the relationship between economy and social structure.

365. Lévi-Strauss, Claude (1969) *The Elementary Structures of Kinship* tr. J.H. Bell and J.R. von Sturmer, R. Needham (ed.), Eyre & Spottiswoode, London. (Beacon Press, Boston – same translation 1969). There is one brief note on p. 259 which compares marriage gifts with kula opening and clinching gifts, however, the sections on exchange and purchase have considerable theoretical importance for an understanding of exchange relations in the kula.

366. Lewis, Albert B. (1929) *Melanesian Shell Money in Field Museum Collections*. Field Museum of Natural History Publication 268, Chicago. General description of manufacture and uses of shell money and decorations in Melanesia. Focus on Melanesia, gives several early German references. Illustrations.
367. Lewis, Albert B. (1932?) *The Melanesians; People of the South Pacific* in *Publications of the Chicago Natural History Museum (Fieldiana): Anthropology Series*, Chicago. Not seen by editor.
368. Lewis, Joan M. (1976) *Social Anthropology in Perspective*. Penguin Books, Harmondsworth, pp. 199-203. Textbook. Based on Malinowski. Description of kula and theories of exchange.
369. Liep, John (1982) 'Ranked exchange in Yela (Rossel Island)', in *The Kula: New Perspectives on Massim Exchange,* Leach, E.R. & Leach, J.W. (eds.) (see item 344). An examination of the exchange of valuables on Rossel Island relating the system to the control of powerful men of processes of production and of social reproduction by the management of marriage payments and exchanges.
370. Liep, John (1979) 'Exchange and social reproduction in the kula region'. Unpublished kula Conference paper. An attempt to situate kula exchange within the more general analysis of the trade network of the region where 'the local modes of existence of widespread populations are combined and made interdependent'.
371. Lithgow, David & Staatsen, Philip (1965) *Languages of the d'Entrecasteaux*. Dept. of Information and Extension Services in Cooperation with the Summer Institute of Linguistics.
372. Lithgow, D.B. (1976) 'Austronesian Languages: Milne Bay and Adjacent Islands', in *New Guinea Area Languages and Language Study*, Wurm, S.A. (ed.), Vol. 2, Canberra.
373. Lithgow, David (1978) 'Present Trends in *Kula* at Dobu'. Unpublished paper. A brief paper by a European kula trader drawing attention to the changes in the methods of exchange since Malinowski. He notes the entry of women; the use of hired motor launches and use of cash to acquire traditional wealth.
374. Lowie, Robert H. (1937) *The History of Ethnological Theory*. Rinehart & Co. Inc., New York, pp. 228-247. Lowie expounds on Malinowski's contributions to the study of anthropology, drawing interesting comparisons with the approach and achievements of Richard Thurnwald.
375. Lyons, A.P. (1925) 'The Significance of the Parental State Amongst Muruans,' in *MAN*, XXV. Unusually sensitive account of Woodlark first-pregnancy rituals and accompanying ideology. Marginal.
376. MacBeath, Alexander (1952) *Experiments in Living*. Macmillan & Co. Ltd.,

London, pp. 126-129, 137, 142, 359. Lecture IV on 'The Way of Life of the Trobriand Islanders'. Involves a description of the kula and the ways in which its values pervade every aspect of Trobriand life.

377. McCarthy, Frederick D. (1947) 'Native Commerce in Oceania', in *Australian Museum Magazine*, Vol. 9, No. 4, pp. 117-120 and Vol. 9, No. 5, pp. 149-152. Not seen by editor.

378. MacCormack, Geoffrey (1976) 'Reciprocity', in *MAN, The Journal of the Royal Anthropological Institute*, Vol. II, No. 1, March, 1967, pp. 89-103. A discussion of the meaning of 'reciprocity in anthropology, aiming at drawing distinctions between description of social phenomena and rules or ideals'. Critical of Malinowski's use of the term.

379. Macintyre, Martha (1979) 'Kune on Tubetube and in the Bwanabwana Region of the Southern Massim', in *The Kula: New Perspectives on Massim Exchange*, Leach, E.R. & Leach, J.W. (eds.) (see item 344).

380. Mair, Lucy (1948) *Australia in New Guinea*. Melbourne University Press, Melbourne. Chapter 1 has very brief reference to the kula as an underlying force in crucial social relations.

381. Mair, Lucy (1965) *An Introduction to Social Anthropology*. Clarendon, Oxford, pp. 160-161, 168, 172, 176, 242. Textbook. The main entry is in the section on 'The Exchange of Goods', where Mair explains the dual functions of kula, as an economic and social institution. Other examples are concerned with kula in respect to neo-classical economic theory.

382. Marett, R.R. (1933) *Sacraments of Simple Folk*, Gifford Lectures, 1932-1933. Clarendon Press, Oxford, pp. 175-177. Refers to Malinowski's and Fortune's accounts of the kula emphasizing the ritual element.

383. Margot-Duclot, Jean & Vernant, Jacques (1946) 'La Terre et la catégorie du sexe en Mélanésie', in *Journal de la Société des Océanistes*, Tome 11, No. 2, décembre, 1946. Marginal.

384. Mauss, Marcel (1923-1924) 'Essai sur le don', in *Année Sociologique*, Deuxième Série, Vol. 1. Reprinted in *Sociologie et Anthropologie*, Mauss, Marcel (see item 385). This classic in anthropology raises most of the theoretical issues still current in economic anthropology. Much of Mauss' material for arguments concerning reciprocity is drawn from Malinowski's *Argonauts.*

385. Mauss, Marcel (1950) *Sociologie et Anthropologie*. Presses Universitaires de France, Paris.

386. Mauss, Marcel (1954) *The Gift*. Translated by Ian Cunnison. Cohen & West, London.

387. Mauss, Marcel (1969) *Oeuvres*, Vol. III. Minuit, Paris.

388. Mead, Margaret (1933) 'More Comprehensive Field Methods', in *American Anthropologist*, N.S., Vol. 35, No. 1, 1933. This article was written after Mead returned from New Guinea and contains reference to Fortune's work

on Dobu, mentioning problems of discovering the kula as a *system*. It is not an important reference, and the article itself is not concerned with conveying any ethnographic information.

389. Montague, Susan (1974) 'The Trobriand Society'. Ph.D. Thesis, Chicago. A study from a Kaileuna perspective.

390. Montague, Susan (1978) 'Church, Government and Western Ways in a Trobriand Village'. Unpublished kula Conference paper. This paper offers a preliminary examination of the role of Christianity and Western government in the social organization of a Trobriand village.

391. Moyne, Lord (1936) *Walkabout*. William Heinemann Ltd., London, pp. 69-76. Introduction by A.C. Haddon. Mention of pottery found in 'tombs'. Of minimal importance. Photographs.

392. Munn, Nancy (1971) 'The Symbolism of Perceptual Qualities: A Study in Trobriand Ritual Aesthetics'. Paper delivered to the American Anthropological Association. An examination of 'Trobriand ritual symbolism from the perspective of its logico-aesthetic structure'. References to the symbolism associated with kula exchange.

393. Munn, Nancy (1972) 'Symbolic Time in the Trobriands of Malinowski's Era: An Essay on the Anthropology of Time'. Unpublished paper. This paper explores the symbolic forms of social time as expressed in a variety of institutions in the Trobriands. Section V deals specially with kula exchange, 'synchronization, delay and timing'.

394. Munn, Nancy (1977) 'The Spatiotemporal Transformations of Gawa Canoes', *Journal de la Société des Océanistes,* T. XXXIII, mars-juin, 1977, pp. 39-51. An examination of the construction and exchange of a Gawan canoe in terms of the symbolism of each stage of the process.

395. Munn, Nancy (1979) 'Gawan *Kula*: Spatiotemporal control and the symbolism of influence', in *The Kula: New Perspectives on Massim Exchange,* Leach, E.R. & Leach, J.W. (eds.) (see item 344). An analysis of kula: 'on the one hand... as a system which constructs a particular kind of inter-island level and mode of Gawan structural space and time; on the other... as a medium through which the actor gains a certain control over this space-time'.

396. Murray, John Hubert Plunkett (1925) *Papua of Today or An Australian Colony in the Making.* King & Son Ltd., London, pp. 244-245. Refers to Malinowski and kula; compares with *Hiri*, trade between Port Moresby and the Gulf of Papua.

397. Nadel, S.F. (1957) 'Malinowski on Magic and Religion', in *Man and Culture,* Firth, R. (ed.) (see item 235), p. 206. Very brief reference to kula myths and actual exchanges.

398. Nash, Manning (1964) 'The Organization of Economic Life', in *Horizons of*

Anthropology, Tax, S. (ed.). Aldine Pub. Co., Chicago, p. 171. Textbook. Situates kula in the Solomon Islands!

399. Naval Intelligence Division, Great Britain (1945) *Pacific Islands, Volume IV - Western Pacific,* (New Guinea and Islands Northward). Chapter XIV mentions kula, but all ethnographic information is derived from Austen, Leo (1936) (see item 69).

400. Neale, Walter C. (1976) *Monies in Societies.* Chandler & Sharp, San Francisco. Marginal. Presents Trobriands as a non-monetary society; kula is mentioned in respect to trade.

401. Nogaro, B. (1935) *La monnaie et les phénomènes monetaires contemporains.* Sirey, Paris. A theoretical work which elaborates the relationship and transformation of commodities and currency.

402. Oakes, Guy (1977) 'Introductory Essay', in *Critique of Stammler*, Weber, Max. (ed.) Free Press, New York, pp. 30-36. Use of kula exchange as example to show some of the logical and sociological properties of the *'verstehen'* approach to social facts. (Secondary analysis.)

403. Oderman, Gisela (1955) 'Der Eingeborenen Handel in der Suedsee', in *Annali Lateranensi*, 18, pp. 319-556. (Indigenous trade in the Pacific). A monograph-length article with a good general survey of trade networks in Oceania. Comparative treatment of various aspects of trade - mainly in the form of accumulation of instances. Numerous references to Massim - esp. pp. 330-333 (general), pp. 394-399 (kula), pp. 441-442 (kula mythology), and pp. 499-501 (affinal exchange). Extensive bibliography.

404. Oliver, Douglas L. (1951) *The Pacific Islands.* Harvard Univ. Press, Cambridge, Mass., p. 40. Brief description of trade, using Tubetube, Dobu and Trobriands to illustrate the pattern of delayed reciprocity and complementarity of valuables. Stresses hedonistic elements in trade.

405. Panoff, Michel (1970) 'Marcel Mauss's *The Gift* Revisited', in *MAN*, N.S. Vol. 5, No. 1, pp. 60-71. A discussion of Mauss' theories of exchange, reciprocity and primitive economics in the light of contemporary theories and criticism of *The Gift*.

406. Panoff, Michel (1972) *Bronislaw Malinowski.* Petite Bibliothèque, Payot, Paris.

407. Parker, R.S. (1971) See under Epstein, A.L. (1971) item 225.

408. Patterson, Mary (1974-1975) 'Sorcery and Witchcraft in Melanesia', in *Oceania,* Vol. XLV, Nos. 2 & 3, p. 144. 'Melanesian witchcraft is confined almost exclusively to a relatively small area which corresponds with that encompassed by the trading expeditions of the kula exchange ring...' Only *females* are witches.

409. Peacock, James L. & Kirsch, Thomas A. (n.d.) *The Human Direction: An Evolutionary Approach to Social and Cultural Anthropology.* Appleton-Century-Crofts, New York. Textbook.

410. Pearson, Harry W. (1958) 'The Economy has no Surplus: Critique of a
Theory of Development', in *Trade and Markets in Early Empires,* Polanyi,
K., Arensberg, C. & Pearson, H.W. (eds.) (see item 420), pp. 320-339.
Involves a discussion of kula in terms of a 'prestige economy' as distinct from
a market economy, where different concepts of wealth and value operate.
411. Perry, W.J. (1935) *The Primordial Ocean: An Introductory Contribution to
Social Psychology.* Methuen, London, 1935, pp. 91-94. No specific mention of the kula but extensive use of *Argonauts.* Focus on Malinowski's
essentially idealist conceptions about the gift relationship.
412. Petri, H. (1936) 'Die Geldformen der Südsee', in *Anthropos,* 31, 1936, pp.
187-212, 509-554. (The forms of money in the Pacific.) A thorough
description and classification of types of 'money' in the Pacific. Concludes
that the oldest forms of 'money' (stone rings and shell money) are
associated with the Austroasian culture originating in S.E. Asia. Describes
Massim 'shell money strings' pp. 531-533 (fig. 18), *Conus* armshells p. 536
(fig. 4), and axe blades pp. 547-548. Extensive bibliography.
413. Pfeiffer, J.E. (1977) See Friedl, J. (1977) item 248.
414. Piddington, Ralph (1950) *An Introduction to Social Anthropology*, Vols. 1
& 2. Oliver & Boyd, Edinburgh, pp. 270-282. Textbook. Exchange and
the kula. A brief outline in functionalist terms, entirely and uncritically
based on Malinowski's analytical conceptions of wealth, exchange and
reciprocity.
415. Piddington, Ralph (1957) 'Malinowski's Theory of Needs', in *Man and
Culture,* Firth, R. (ed.) (see item 235), p. 48. The kula presented as a
response to 'various derived and integrative responses'.
416. Pi-Sunyer, Oriol & Salzmann, Zdenek, (n.d. [?1978]) *Humanity & Culture
An Introduction to Anthropology.* Houghton Mifflin Co., Boston. Textbook. Based on Sahlins and Malinowski, discusses the social value of the
kula as a system of redistribution.
417. Pöch, R. (1907) 'Einige bemerkenswerte Ethnologika aus Neu Guinea', in
Mitteilungen der Anthropologischen Gesellschaft in Wein, 37, 1907, pp.
57-71, 125. (Some remarkable ethnographical objects from New Guinea.)
Records various objects collected by the author in New Guinea 1904-
1906. Includes a report of an excavation of refuse heaps in Wanigela,
Collingwood Bay with sherds of decorated pottery, burials, and a carved
Conus shell - illustrations, pp. 69-70.
418. Polanyi, Karl (1944) *The Great Transformation.* Rinehart & Co. Inc., New
York. Theoretically important.
419. Polanyi, Karl (1953) *Semantics of General Economic History.* New York,
Columbia University Research Project on 'Origins of Economic Institutions',
pp. 161-184. Reprinted as 'Anthropology and Economic Theory', in *Readings in Anthropology,* Vol II, Fried, M. (ed.). Crowell, New York, 1959, pp.

161-184. Textbook. In discussing personal reciprocity, Polanyi refers to Malinowski's idea that reciprocative behaviour 'rests on symmetrical forms of basic social organization'. Stress on social integration.

420. Polanyi, Karl, Arensberg, C. & Pearson, H.W. (eds.) (1958) *Trade and Markets in the Early Empires.* The Free Press, New York, pp. 243-270, 320-341, 342-356. This collection of essays is a seminal work in the development of substantivist economic theory as applied in anthropology. Although there are only three direct references to kula many of the articles discuss general issues such as 'monetization', 'reciprocity', etc. and by implication the kula is brought in – the work of Malinowski is more often referred to, in particular his antagonism towards the idea of 'economic man' and his influence in the discipline generally. See entries for Polanyi, K. (items 418-421) and Pearson, H.W. (item 410).

421. Polanyi, Karl (1958) 'The Economy as Instituted Process', in *Trade and Markets in Early Empires,* Polanyi, K., Arensberg, C. & Pearson, H.W. (eds.) (see item 420), pp. 243-270. Reprinted in *Economic Anthropology – Readings in Theory and Analysis*, LeClair, Edward & Schneider, Harold (eds.) (see item 352). This article is general and theoretical with implicit and explicit references to the kula from a substantivist view. Kula discussed in terms of 'Reciprocity, Redistribution and Exchange'.

422. Powell, H.A. (1957). An Analysis of Present-Day Social Structure in the Trobriand Islands. (Unpublished) Ph.D. Thesis, University of London.

423. Powell, H.A. (1960) 'Competitive Leadership in Trobriand Political Organization', in *Journal of the Royal Anthropological Institute,* 90, pp. 131ff. Not directly relevant to kula, but his conclusions have been drawn on by others in discussion of kula exchange, prestige and ranking on Trobriands.

424. Powell, H.A. (1969) 'Territory, hierarchy and kinship in Kiriwina', in *MAN,* Vol. 4, No. 4. Mainly concerned with kinship relations, but contains a long discussion on the significance of *urigubu* which is relevant to Weiner's studies of the meanings of yam exchange on the Trobriands.

425. Powell, H.A. (1976) 'The Trobriand Experiment', film review, in *R.A.I.N., Royal Anthropological Institute News,* March/April, 1976.

426. Powell, Harry A. (1978) 'The *Kula* in Trobriand Politics'. Unpublished kula Conference paper. A discussion of the institutions of leadership in the Trobriands and in particular the semi-hereditary 'Big men' and their involvement in kula.

427. Powys, Erich (1958) *A Teacher's Book of Social Studies,* for Standards 3 to 6. Jacaranda Press, Brisbane. Textbook. The kula briefly described. School textbook.

428. Preble, E. (1962) See Kardiner, A. (1962) item 320.

429. Quiggan, A. Hingston (1949) *A Survey of Primitive Money.* Methuen, London, pp. 18, 172-174. Presents kula as an emergent 'currency'. Based on

Seligmann, suggests that *beku* and spatulae change in value as they move south and then 'may be described as currency'. Interestingly is the only source which correctly says that *bagi* are made of *Chama pacificus* (more usual than *Spondylus*). Discusses use of shell valuables in death payments and bridewealth. Contains photographs.

430. Quiggan, A.H. (1956) *The Story of Money*. Methuen, London, pp. 6, 22. A popular book for the lay reader. General survey of types of money. No direct reference to kula but information in sections on 'Present Giving and Gift Exchange' and 'Shell Money'.

431. Radin, Paul (1953) *The World of Primitive Man*. H. Schumran Inc., New York, pp. 117, 126-132. Based on Malinowski and Fortune, discusses kula as economic activity, critical of Malinowski's stress on non-utility of exchange. Textbook.

432. Reay, Marie (1963) Review of Uberoi, J.P. Singh, *Politics of the Kula Ring*, in *Oceania*, Vol. 33, No. 4, June, pp. 296-298.

433. Reay, M. (1971) See Epstein, A.L. (1971) item 225.

434. Rey, P.H.P. (1968, 1973) See Dupré, G. (1968, 1973) items 217-218.

435. Rivers, W.H.R. (1926) 'Trade, Warfare and Slavery', in *Psychology and Ethnology*, Elliot Smith, G. (ed.). Kegan Paul, Trench, Trubner & Co. Ltd., London. This short article is important as it constitutes one of the first responses to Malinowski's *Argonauts*. (As Rivers died in 1922, it represents one of his last writings. An interesting example of the response of the 'establishment' anthropologist to Malinowski.) Rivers accepts Malinowski's interpretation but does state that similar, entirely utilitarian trade institutions existed elsewhere in Melanesia - p. 293. Reads like a lecture, and although the preface suggests that it might have been previously published, no trace of earlier publication can be found and the paper does not exist in any form in the St John's Collection, nor in the Haddon Library, Cambridge.

436. Robinson, Marguerite S. (1962) 'Complementary Filiation and Marriage in the Trobriand Islands: A re-examination of Malinowski's Material', in *Marriage in Tribal Societies*, Fortes, Meyer (ed.), Cambridge University Press, pp. 121-155. Mainly concerned with kinship, marriage and the 'jural significance of the father in Trobriand paternal, marital and affinal relations'. Lengthy examination of exchanges related to marriage involving the transfer of valuables. Cites Malinowski (1935) in relation to marriage between Sineketans and Kiriwinans where the former produce valuable shell ornaments which are exchanged in marriage and used for kula trade. Useful for comparison with *Women of Value, Men of Renown*, Weiner, Annette (1976) (see item 523).

437. Rogers, E.S. (1970) *New Guinea: Big Man Island*. Royal Ontario Museum, pp. 80-105, see particularly Chapter V, 'Island Traders'. Contains map of the kula with some of the additional trade routes between the kula ring

and the mainland and indicating trade in other items, pottery, canoes, stone axe blades and wooden articles as well as food and clay. Notes differences in use of kula items on Dobu and dependence on other imports in kula (e.g. axes to Trobriands). Stresses dual/multiple functions – economic, political – 'makes for peaceful relations between essentially hostile groups'. Notes that items escape the circuit as *valuables*. General ethnographic summaries and excellent photographs of artefacts – lime spatulae, necklaces, carved canoe prow, wooden weapons, axes.

438. Roheim, Geza (1923) 'Heiliges Geld in Melanesien', in *Internationale Zeitschrift für Psychoanalyse,* IX, 1923. On the symbolism of kula objects.

439. Roheim, Geza (1937) 'Death and Mourning Ceremonies at Normanby Island', in *MAN*, Vol. 37, pp. 49-50. An appallingly cryptic summary of a communication. There is a line on p. 50: 'Death and the *'une'* (*kula*); the dead are departed, those who have sailed'.

440. Roheim, Geza (1946) 'Yaboaine, a War God of Duau', in *Oceania*, Vol. XVI, 1946, pp. 217, 220-222, 320, 325. Mainly concerned with myth of a warrior hero, but includes considerable detail on the memories of war and cannibalism. References to the use of kula objects in exchanges for human flesh.

441. Roheim, Geza (1950) *Psychoanalysis and Anthropology*, International Universities Press (reprinted 1968) New York, pp. 183-203. Gives an example of the ways in which kula partnerships can be begun, by delaying repayment or making a valuable. Gives brief versions of Kasabwaibwaileta myth from Duau and Fergusson, Dobu and Widiwidi. Speculates on the social origins of the kula and the psychological symbolism of myths and objects.

442. Roheim, Geza (1954) 'Cannibalism in Duau, Normanby Island, D'Entrecasteaux Group, Territory of Papua', in *Mankind*, Vol. IV, No. 12, pp. 488-492. An important article containing Roheim's ideas about the relationship between *kune* (kula) exchange and war, cannibalism and the establishment of peace. Based on discussions and evidence from myths. Roheim's Normanby material and the Rossel Island examples suggest that formerly entrance to the kula might have been possible through killing an enemy and exchanging the flesh for valuables, see especially pp. 489-490.

443. Rosman, A. (n.d. & 1978) See Rubel, P. (n.d. & 1978) items 446-447.

444. Rossi, Ino, Buettner-Janusch, John, Coppenhauer, Dorian (eds.) (1977) *Anthropology in Full Circle.* Praeger Publishers, New York, pp. 272-276. Textbook. Quote *from Argonauts* (pp. 81-83 and 91-95) headed: 'The Essentials of the Kula'.

445. Rowley, C.D. (1971) 'Social Change', in *Papua New Guinea. Prospero's Other Island*, Dundas, Kerry and others (eds.). Angus & Robertson,

Sydney, pp. 91–92. Based on Malinowski and Fortune, brief description and reference to the kula and its social force – the extension of mutual obligations outside the small village community.

446. Rubel, Paula & Rosman, Abraham (n.d.) 'Exchange Partners in New Guinea Societies', in *Information*, 14:5, 1975, pp. 65–79. Also in *Human Societies and Ecosystems* (n.d.). Of comparative and theoretical relevance. Argues for a comparative structural analysis of marriage rules and commodity exchange relationships.

447. Rubel, Paula & Rosman, Abraham (1978) *Your Own Pigs You May Not Eat. A Comparative Study of New Guinea Societies.* The University of Chicago Press. A wide-ranging study of ceremonial exchange relying on both structuralism and exchange theory. One brief comparative reference to kula, p. 336.

448. Rumens, John (1972) 'Milne Bay District', in *Encyclopaedia of Papua New Guinea*, Ryan, P. (gen. ed.), Vol. 2, pp. 763–771. Overview of Milne Bay – Massim area with data on population, administration, geography, income, history.

449. Sady, R.R. (1969) *Perspectives from Anthropology.* Teachers College Press, Columbia University, New York, pp. 37–38. Textbook. Kula mentioned as a system of social networks in chapter on 'Diversity of Cultures'.

450. Sahlins, Marshall D. (1960) 'Political Power and the Economy in Primitive Society: the Trobriands', in *Essays in the Science of Culture*, Dole, G.E. & Camiero, R.L. (eds.). Crowell, New York, pp. 405–407. Textbook. Discussion of the social and economic functions of chieftainship in the Trobriands, emphasizing the ways in which 'economic relations are embedded in a kinship structure'.

451. Sahlins, Marshall, D. (1965) 'On the Sociology of Primitive Exchange', in *The Relevance of Models for Social Anthropology*, Gluckman, M., Eggan, F. & Banton, M. (eds.). A.S.A. Monograph 1. Reprinted as Chapter 5 of *Stone Age Economics*, Sahlins, Marshall (1974) (see item 455). Textbook.

452. Sahlins, Marshall (1965) 'Exchange-value and the Diplomacy of Primitive Trade', in *Essays in Economic Anthropology*, Helm, June (ed.). A.E.S. Proceedings, Seattle. Early version of Chapter 6, *Stone Age Economics*, Sahlins, Marshall (1974) (see item 455).

453. Sahlins, Marshall (1968) 'Philosophie politique de *l'Essai sur le don*', in *L'Homme*, Vol. 8 [4], 1968, pp. 5–17. Discussion of Mauss' theory of reciprocity.

454. Sahlins, Marshall (1969) 'The Spirit of the Gift', in *Echanges et communications*, Pouillon, J. & Maranda, P. (eds.). Mouton, The Hague. Rewritten and expanded as Chapter 4 in *Stone Age Economics*, Sahlins

Marshall (1974) (see item 455). A discussion of Mauss' theory of obligation and reciprocity as presented in *The Gift*.

455. Sahlins, Marshall (1974) *Stone Age Economics*. Tavistock Publications, London, 1974. Textbook. This collection of six essays discusses the kula and primitive trade in several contexts. The volume deals with theoretical aspects of exchange in terms of theories of reciprocity, the role of exchange in ranked or stratified societies and the relation between 'economic' and 'social' obligation in anthropological theory. It is a major contribution to substantivist economics in anthropology and has been an important influence in recent discussions of trade, exchange and economic relations.

456. Salisbury, R.F. (1962) *From Stone to Steel*. Melbourne University Press, Melbourne, pp. 197–200. This book is mainly concerned with the impact of European goods and money on the Siane economy. However, the chapter 'Economic Values' includes a discussion of the kula in terms of the debates on money and spheres of exchange. Salisbury comes down firmly in Malinowski's camp – the kula items are not commodities in ordinary economic activities.

457. Salisbury, Richard F. (1966) 'Politics and Shell-Money Finance in New Britain', in *Political Anthropology*, Swartz, M.J., Turner, V.W. & Tuden, A. (eds.) (see item 496), p. 113. Textbook. Brief mention of kula as a ceremonial trading system which reflects and is the key to social mobility and political power.

458. Salzmann, Zdenek, (n.d.) See Pi-Sunyer, Oriol (n.d.) item 416.

459. Saville, W.J.V. (1926) *In Unknown New Guinea*. Seeley Service & Co. Ltd., London, pp. 110–167. Introduction by Malinowski. This section of an ethnographic study of Mailu contains detailed and unique information about the production of armshells, trade and trade routes, the changes during the first part of this century due to European intervention and the nature of Mailu trade partnerships.

460. Saxe, A.A. (1977) See Gall, P.L. (1977) item 252.

461. Scheffler, Harold W. (1965) 'Big Men and Disks of Shell: Political Finance in Melanesia', in *Natural History,* December, 1965. Kula as an example of an institution dominated by powerful men who use the exchange of valuables to enhance their prestige. Mistakenly refers to *mwali* and *bagi* as 'kula'. Article is general and comparative – concerning many types of shell valuables.

462. Schlesier, Erhard (1964) 'Me'udana (Normanby Island)', Fest zum Abschluss der Trauerzeit (bwabware)'. Film E534 der Encyclopaedia Cinematographica. 11 pp. Goettingen. An accompanying leaflet to the Film 'Feast marking the end of the mourning period (bwabware)', deals with food-exchange relations.

463. Schlesier, E. (1965) 'Sagogewinnung auf Normanby Island, Südost Neu-guinea', in *Baessler Archiv*, NF XIII, pp. 1-39. (Taken from Crosby (1976) [item 200] bibliography/contents unknown.)

464. Schlesier, Erhard (1967) 'Sagari-Tanze'. Film E535 der Encyclopaedia Cinematographica. 9 pp. Goettingen. This is an accompanying leaflet to the film *'Sagari Dances'. Sagari* (Trobriand *Sagali*) is connected with food exchange relations.

465. Schlesier, Erhard (1968) 'Zum Bootbau auf Normanby Island, Neuguinea', in *Baessler Archiv*, Vol. 16. Berlin, pp. 129-135. Contains remarks on canoe manufacture on Normanby Island.

466. Schlesier, Erhard (1970) *Me'udana (Südost-Neuguinea). Teil I: Die soziale Struktur.* Albert Limbach Verlag, Braunschweig, 1970, 93 pp. (Me'udana (Southeast New Guinea). Part I: The social structure. Structural-functional analysis of the social structure of an inland group of eastern Normanby Island. Analysis of structure and history of settlements and descent groups, kinship behaviour and terminology. Analysis of social organization to be published separately. Mentions acquisition of land rights by payment of *bagi* and *mwali*, p. 41. Map of Normanby, p. 12. (Volume II, which is in preparation, contains an exposition of the *Sagari* (memorial feast and food exchange cycle) which in its special form at Me'udana is considered by the author to be a substitute for kula in the mountain area.)

467. Schneider, D.M. (1963) Review of Uberoi, J.P. Singh, *Politics of the Kula Ring*, in *American Sociological Review*, Vol. 28, June, p. 501.

468. Schneider, Harold (1968) See LeClair, Edward (1968) item 352.

469. Schneider, Harold K. (1974) *Economic Man: The Anthropology of Economics.* The Free Press. Not seen by editor.

470. Schneider, O. (1905) *Muschelgeld Studien.* Dresden, 1905, 190 pp. (Shell money studies.) A posthumous, unfinished manuscript. Survey of forms of shell money in Oceania and Africa. Very limited treatment of New Guinea. Mentions shell valuables in southeast New Guinea and Massim pp. 66-68.

471. Schott, Rudiger (1958) 'Die Eigentumsrechte der Trobriand-Insulaner in Nordwest-Melanesien', in *Anthropos*, 53, 1958, pp. 88-135. ('The Rights of Ownership Among Trobriand Islanders of North Western Melanesia'.)

472. Schwartz, B. (1967) 'The Social Psychology of the Gift', in *American Journal of Sociology*, Vol. 73, No. 1. A theoretical article discussing gift-giving as a means of promoting social equilibrium.

473. Schwartz, T. (1963) 'Systems of areal integration', in *Anthropological Forum*, 1, pp. 56-98. See p. 89.

474. Schwimmer, E. (1973) *Exchange in the Social Structure of the Orokaiwa.* C. Hurst & Co., London. A detailed ethnographical analysis of exchange and reciprocity. Schwimmer's interests in Malinowski's theories of myth

and ceremonial exchange are referred to and are acknowledged as a major influence in an otherwise transactionalist approach. No explicit comparison with kula.

475. Schwimmer, Erick (1977) 'What is Exchange Theory?', in *Reviews in Anthropology*, March/April, 1977, pp. 189–209. Review essay on Heath, A. (1976) (see item 285) and Kapferer, B. (1976) *Transaction and Meaning: Directions in the Anthropology of Exchange and Symbolic Behaviour,* I.S.H.I., Philadelphia; outlining the main trends in exchange theory from Malinowski to the present day. A very good bibliography on the subject.

476. Scoditti, G.G. (1978) *Kitava: Iconologia e Semantica*. Einaudi, Torino (Turin).

477. Scoditti, Giancarlo (1978) 'The *Kula*: a scenic performance of *Monikiniki,* the mythical hero'. Unpublished Kula Conference paper. A paper which explores the relationship between a mythical hero and his activities, the representation of this myth in the iconography of canoe carvings and the relationship of the myth to the regular enactment of kula voyages.

478. Scoditti, Giancarlo (1979) '*Kula* on Kitava', in *The Kula: New Perspectives on Massim Exchange,* Leach, E.R. & Leach, J.W. (eds.) (see item 344). Basic ethnographic data on Kitavan kula, based on fieldwork during the period 1973–1976. Deals with participation, entry into kula, the trading districts and their links to east and west and kula symbolism.

479. Seagle, William (1937) 'Primitive Law and Professor Malinowski', in *American Anthropologist,* N.S. 39, 193, pp. 275ff. Review article of *Crime and Custom in Savage Society.* Several sections deal with Malinowski's notions of reciprocity and obligation.

480. Seligmann, C.G. (1906) *The Melanesians of British New Guinea.* Cambridge University Press. This classic study contains a considerable amount of data on production and distribution throughout the Massim, with most of the data coming from the southern islands. The sections on 'Property and Inheritance' and 'Trade' contain a discussion of wealth items and 'currency' which indicates that Seligmann was aware of most elements of the kula trade. The section on the stone axe blades suggests that there was a further decline between 1908 and the period when Malinowski was in the Massim. See also the entry for Barton, F.R. (1910) (item 145).

481. Seligmann, C.G. & Strong, W. Mersh (1910) 'Anthropogeographical investigations in British New Guinea', in *The Geographical Journal,* Vol. XXVII, No. 3, pp. 225–242, 347–369. Pre-Malinowski. Describes visit to the stone quarry of Sulogo and Murua where stone tools, *benam* (Tube-tube word for beku, stone axe blade) were formerly made, manufacture having been abandoned two generations previously (1906). Mentions export of *benam*, which, together with armshells, constitute a high-denomina-

tion currency which has increased in value and has retained ceremonial usage and the prestige associated with possession.

482. Service, Elman R. (1958) *Profiles in Ethnology*. Harper & Row, New York, pp. 229-249. This is a brief survey of the history of anthropology, presumably meant as an introduction to the subject. The material on the kula (pp. 233-236) is derived from Malinowski entirely and stresses the functions dealing with social relations.

483. Sider, Karen Blu (1967) 'Affinity and the role of the father in the Trobriands', in *Southwestern Journal of Anthropology*, 23, pp. 90-109. This article is a discussion of paternity in the kinship system based on Malinowski's, Powell's and Robinson's studies of Trobriand fatherhood. Kula is mentioned briefly with respect to competition for rank within a village.

484. Simmons, Alan (1931) 'Sex among the Savages', in *Anthropos*, Vol. 31, No. 2, pp. 61-62. Review of Malinowski, B. *The Sexual Life of Savages*.

485. Sloan, William N. (1973) 'Valuables and Vegetables: an Alliance Theory Investigation of Trobriand Society', in *Journal of Symbolic Anthropology*, No.2, September, 1973. Mouton, The Hague.

486. Smelsner, N. (1959) 'A Comparative View of Exchange Systems'. Review of Polanyi, K., Arensberg, C., Pearson, H., *Trade and Markets in the Early Empires*, in *Economic Development*, Vol. 7, pp. 173-182.

487. Smith, Robin & Willey, Keith (1969) *New Guinea*. Lansdowne, Melbourne. Photographs throughout text. Text, pp.110-119. Carving a wooden bowl for trade, Boitalu village, Trobriands, p.36. Very inaccurate notes on kula on p. 114.

488. Spain, D.H. (1975) *Readings in Sociocultural Anthropology*. The Dorsey Press, Illinois. Kula, pp. 107-108. Reprint of Scheffler, Harold article 'Big Men and Disks of Shell', (see item 461).

489. Specht, Jim & White, Peter J. (1978) 'Trade and Exchange in Oceania and Australia', in *Mankind*, 11 (3). Sydney University Press. This special edition of *Mankind* is a collection of papers delivered at the 1977 symposium on trade and exchange in Australia and the Pacific Islands. See also the entries for Weiner, A. (1978) (item 526), Harding, T. (1978) (item 275) and Egloff, B.J. (1978) (item 554).

490. Staatsen, P. (1965) See Lithgow, D. (1965) item 371.

491. Stanner, W.E. (1933-1934) 'Ceremonial Economics of the Mulluk Mulluk and Madngella Tribes of the Daly River, Northern Australia', in *Oceania*, Vol. 4, pp. 156-175, 468-471. A discussion of aboriginal exchange where Stanner seems to 'stretch' the ceremonial aspects of the trade to draw parallels with the kula. (See Lauer, P.K. (1970) item 337). In view of Lauer's work, it now appears that there may be more similarities between

such exchange and kula. Bibliography of other, similar institutions in Australia, useful for comparison.

492. Steiner, Franz (1954) 'Notes on Comparative Economics', in *British Journal of Sociology*, Vol. 5, pp. 118–129. Notes 'translation' of objects in terms of 'use value' and 'ritual value', kula and *gimwali*.

493. Strathern, Andrew (1979) 'The *Kula* in comparative perspective', in *The Kula: New Perspectives on Massim Exchange*, Leach, E.R. & Leach, J.W. (eds.) (see item 344). Analytical comparison between kula and the ceremonial exchange systems of the Melpa and Enga in the Highlands, the peoples of the Vitiaz Straits and the Huon Gulf, the Tolai, and the Solomons. Focusses on gain-orientation and conversions within systems.

494. Strong, W. Mersh (1906) See Seligmann, C.G. (1906) item 480.

495. Swartz, D.K. (1976) See Jordan, D.K. (1976) item 316.

496. Swartz, M.J., Turner, V.W., & Tuden, A. (eds.) (1966) *Political Anthropology*. Aldine, Chicago, p. 113. Textbook. Brief reference to kula.

497. Tambiah, S.J. (1979) 'On flying witches, and flying canoes: the coding of male and female values' in *The Kula: New Perspectives on Massim Exchange*, Leach, E.R. & Leach, J.W. (eds.) (see item 344). An examination of the logic of Trobriand beliefs on the intrinsic male and female qualities as expressed in the sexual division of labour, the ascription of superhuman capacities and the complementarity of male and female roles which makes kula a quintessential male activity.

498. Taylor, R.B. (1976) *Cultural Ways – A Concise Edition of Introduction to Cultural Anthropology*. Allyn and Bacon Inc., Boston, pp. 141–142. Textbook. Map. Presented in section dealing with distribution and exchange. Briefly notes distinction between kula and barter.

499. Thilenius, G. *Primitives Geld*. (1921) Archiv fur Anthropologie n.F., 18, pp. 1–34, (Primitive money.) Analysis of evolution of money with discussion of earlier contributions (Andrée, Schurtz, etc.). Author distinguishes between natural and cultural money (Naturgeld/Kulturgeld) and among the former between money as good (Nutzgeld) and money as token (Zeichengeld). Coins, which are cultural money, represent the highest development of primitive money. Mentions payment of canoes with axe blades in Deboyne Islands, p. 19 (after Macgregor).

500. Thomson, Donald F. (1949) *Economic Structure and the Ceremonial Exchange Cycle in Arnhem Land*. Macmillan, London, kula, pp. 1, 8. Malinowski's study provided the theoretical base for this examination of ceremonial gift exchange. It is therefore of interest for comparison and influence of Malinowski's ideas of reciprocity, economic interest, etc.

501. Thune, Carl (1978) 'Shells and Civilization: the construction of the kula and personal identity by one Normanby Island Trader'. Unpublished Kula

Conference paper. An examination of the meaning of kula exchange, socially and personally, for one participant on Normanby Island.

502. Thune, Carl E. (1979) *'Kula* traders and lineage members: the structure of village and kula exchange on Normanby Island', in *The Kula: New Perspectives on Massim Exchange,* Leach, E.R. & Leach, J.W. (eds.) (see item 344). An examination of the various exchange systems, both internal and external, and the ways in which valuables can be deployed to establish and re-inforce social relations on Duau. Involves an assessment of historical transformation of exchange, in particular the democratization of the kula following pacification by the British.

503. Thurnwald, R. (1932) *Economics in Primitive Communities.* O.U.P., London, pp. 147-148. Textbook. Stresses distinction between kula and barter by referring to kula as a 'game'. In summarizing Malinowski, he distorts the image, e.g.: 'kula friendships generally inherited'. 'They form the principle theme of tribal gossip.' In section on 'Forms of Economic Activity', hence descriptive emphasis.

504. Tuden, A. (1966) See Swartz, M.J. (1966) item 496.

505. Tueting, Laura Thompson (1935) *Native Trade in Southeast New Guinea.* Bishop Museum, Occasional Papers, Vol. II, No. 15, pp. 1-43. Massim Trade – both barter and ceremonial trade examined mainly concerned with the geographical aspects and with the trading items. Succinct and thorough outline based on published material prior to 1935. Comprehensive bibliography.

506. Turner, V.W. (1966) See Swartz, M.J. (1966) item 496.

507. Uberoi, J.P. Singh (1962) *Politics of the Kula Ring.* Manchester Univ. Press, Manchester. A re-analysis of Seligmann's,Malinowski's and Fortune's publications of the Massim attempting to explain the social and political systems which form the basis for kula and attempting to show how kula 'brings separate and distinct groups into a larger political association'.

508. Uberoi, J.P. Singh (1969) 'Kula', *Encyclopedia of Papua New Guinea*, Vol. 1. p.584. Melbourne University Press.

509. Van Emst, P. (1955) *Geld in Melanesie*, Drukkerij Vos de Swart & Co., Beverwijk (in Dutch).

510. Vayda, A.P. (1961) 'A re-examination of north-west coast economic systems', in *Transactions of the New York Academy of Science,* Ser. 2, 23, pp. 618-624. Although not directly related to the kula this article presents a critique of Mauss which has implications for a theoretical study of kula.

511. Vayda, A.P. (1967) 'On the anthropological study of economies', in *Journal of Economic Studies,* No. 1, pp. 86-90. Discusses the problems surrounding analysis of exchange systems in terms of economics.

512. Vernant, Jacques (1946) See Margot-Duclot, Jean (1946) item 383.

513. Viljoen, Stephan (1936) *The Economics of Primitive Peoples.* Staples Press Ltd., London, pp. 214-217. Brief but early reference to Malinowski's and Mauss' ideas on reciprocity and the relationship between economic and social obligations. Kula is compared with several other trade systems.

514. Voget, F. (1976) *A History of Ethnology.* Holt, Rinehart & Winston Inc., New York, pp. 423-524. Main source is Malinowski, but interprets kula.

515. Waligórski, Andrzej (1967) Epilogue to the Polish translation of *Argonauts,* in Malinowski, B. *Argonauci Zachodniego Pacyfiku.* PWN, Warsaw, pp. 605-645. Reprinted in *Przegląd Socjologiczny,* Vol. XXVIII, 1976, pp. 268-300.

516. Waligórski, Andrzej (1973) *Antropologiczna koncepcja człowieka.* (The Anthropological Concept of Man.) PWN, Warsaw. Contains some references to the kula.

517. Walker, K.F. (1942) 'The Study of Primitive Economics', in *Oceania,* Vol. XIII, December, 1942. Review article referring to kula briefly in relation to problem of 'primitive money'.

518. Warnotte, D. (1927) *Les Origines sociologiques de l'obligation contractuelle.* Institute Solvay, Lamertin, Brussels. Not seen by editor.

519. Watson, Lepani & Groves, M. (1956) 'Trobriand Island Clans & Chiefs. Index of the Permanent Position of Chiefs', letter in *MAN,* Vol. 56, November, p. 164. Letter from a Trobriander correcting Malinowski's material of the chiefs of the Trobriand Islands. Mentions that the chief paid his 'relatives' for work in 'black stone, armshells and money stringshells'.

520. Wedgwood, Camilla (1932) 'The Economic Life in Melanesia', abstract of a paper read at a meeting of the Human Biology Research Committee of the R.A.I., 11 March 1932 in *MAN,* April, 1932, p. 95.

521. Wedgewood, Camilla H. (1953) See Hogbin, H.I. (1953) item 298.

522. Weiner, Annette (1974) 'Women of Value: The main road of exchange in Kiriwina, Trobriand Islands'. Ph.D. Thesis, Bryn Mawr.

523. Weiner, Annette (1976) *Women of Value, Men of Renown - New Perspectives in Trobriand Exchange.* University of Texas Press, pp. 6, 24, 33, 34, 77-79, 91, 109, 128-129, 152, 180-183, 217-218, 232. This study is primarily concerned with internal exchange. However, it includes brief discussion of changes in trading since Malinowski's visit and useful insights into the whole complex of 'valuables', revealing some of the varied uses of items which Malinowski only associated with the kula. Weiner's material reveals that kula items can be taken in or out of the kula, that *bagi* can be broken up and valuables acquired in the kula can be used in yam exchanges, in marriage and as gifts for nurturing, etc. As kula is a male activity, Weiner's arguments about male/female domains and sex-

ually differentiated exchange systems contain important and unique information about the meaning attached to kula.

524. Weiner, Annette (1977) 'Never Split a Brother-Sister Sibling Set: Trobriand Kinship from Another View'. Unpublished. p. 17. Prohibition on kula during mourning ceremonies. Otherwise totally concerned with kinship relations and male/female domains.

525. Weiner, Annette (1977) 'Trobriand Descent: Female/Male Domains', in special issue of *Ethos* in memory of A. Irving Hallowell, Vol. 5, No. 1, Spring, 1977. Argues for the separation of spheres of power. Although no mention of kula, detailed aspects of male power associated with control over material world and certain objects of exchange.

526. Weiner, Annette (1978) 'The Reproductive Model in Trobriand Society', in *Mankind*, Special Issue: The Australian Museum 150th Symposium: Exchange in the Pacific, Vol. 11, No. 3, pp. 175-186. A critique of utilitarian or functional approaches to exchange in terms of Trobriand exchange, stressing the cultural aspects of the reproductive cycle. Contains important information on the relationship between yams and other forms of wealth.

527. Weiner, Annette (1978) 'Epistemology and Ethnographic Reality: A Trobriand Island Case Study', in *American Anthropologist*, Vol. 80, No. 3, September, 1978, pp. 752-757. A discussion of several films on the Trobriands in terms of the concept of ethnographic 'reality', mentions the portrayals of kula on film.

528. Weiner, Annette (1979) 'A world of made is not a world of born: doing kula in Kiriwina', in *The Kula: New Perspectives on Massim Exchange*, Leach, E.R. & Leach, J.W. (eds.) (see item 344). A critical evaluation of some of the concepts derived from Malinowski's kula with its emphasis on reciprocity and a restricted notion of wealth and value. A crucial examination of the processes of kula as transformations of other internal exchanges and social obligations.

529. Weschler, J.C. (1971) See Langness, L.L. (1971) item 335.

530. White, Leslie A. (1959) *The Evolution of Culture.* McGraw-Hill Book Co., New York. Textbook. Kula and economic exchange.

531. Whitten, P. (1976 & 1977) See Hunter, D. (1976 & 1977) items 307 and 308.

532. Wild, B. (1972) See Burns, T. (1972) item 178.

533. Wilden, Anthony (1968) *The Language of the Self.* Johns Hopkins, Baltimore, more, pp. 35, 120. Discussion of symbols and exchange.

534. Wilden, Anthony (1972) *System and Structure. Essays in Communication and exchange.* Tavistock, London, pp. 255-257. The kula as symbolic Exchange – emphasizes kula exchange as means of communication between different systems – 'geographic, linguistic, cultural ...'.

535. Willey, Keith (1969) See Smith, Robin (1969) item 487.
536. Williams, F.E. (1936) *Papuans of the Trans-fly.* Clarendon Press, Oxford, p. 167. A very brief comparative reference to the kula and functions of exchange in Papua. 'They serve to bring the groups concerned into closer connection with one another; they establish relations and confirm them.'
537. Williams, Ronald G. (1972) *The United Church in Papua, New Guinea, and the Solomon Islands.* Trinity Press, Rabaul, Papua New Guinea, pp. 184, 185, 191, 193.
538. Young, Michael (1971) *Fighting with Food.* Cambridge University Press, Cambridge, p. 6. Goodenough Island. Notes the 'relatively undeveloped trade relations with neighbouring societies'. Canoes made for war and short trading trips. 'Shell valuables were obtained (principally from Amphlett Island traders) by barter for pigs and yams.' 'Large proportion of population lived inland. . . excluded from sea trading' (p.15). Festival cycle involving food exchange 'as important to Goodenough Islanders as the kula is to some other Massim societies' (p. 228). Conclusion (pp. 254–264) raises the issue of the effects of pacification on native exchange activities. Malinowski (1935), p. 456 had argued that 'Kula. . . is to a large extent a surrogate and substitute for head-hunting and war.' Young maintains that on Goodenough '. . . peace not merely "permitted" the elaboration of food exchanges, but given the cultural premises, virtually necessitated it' (p. 256). This study presents a crucial argument about the changing nature and role of exchange in Massim society, taking up arguments presented earlier by Salisbury and Berndt in respect to European intervention in New Guinea societies.
539. Young, Michael W. (1971) 'Goodenough Island Cargo Cults', in *Oceania*, Vol. XLII, No. 1, September, 1971. Mentions absence of kula in spite of geographical position.
540. Young, Michael W. (1972) 'Trobriand Islanders', in *Peoples of the World*, Vol. 1, *Australia and Melanesia*, pp. 100–105. Tom Stacey, London. (ed. E.E. Evans-Pritchard). Brief ethnographic description for a lay readership. Colour photographs of kula objects and canoe.
541. Young, Michael W. (1979) 'Ceremonial Visiting in Goodenough Island', in *The Kula: New Perspectives on Massim Exchange,* Leach, E.R. & Leach, J.W. (eds.) (see item 344). An examination of the exchange institutions on Goodenough involving solicitation of goods, particularly food. These institutions are analogous to kula, serving similar economic and political functions and the behaviour of traders is governed by the same notions of propriety and social obligation.
542. Young, Michael W. (1979) 'The theme of the resentful hero: stasis and mobility in Goodenough mythology', in *The Kula: New Perspectives on*

Massim Exchange, Leach, E.R. & Leach, J.W. (eds.) (see item 344). A comparative analysis of several myths, including the Kasabwaybwayreta myth discussed by Malinowski as a kula myth. A common theme is 'the essential duplicity of exchange...the ambivalence and ambiguity of giving and receiving things of value...' and a recurrent image is that of stasis or retention compared, explicitly or implicitly, with mobility and extravagance.

543. Young, Michael (ed.) (1979) *The Ethnography of Malinowski*. Routledge & Kegan Paul, London, pp. 159-204. Selections from Malinowski's work on the Trobriand Islands with an introduction by the editor.

Archaeological Material

545. Allen, Jim (1977) 'Sea traffic, trade and expanding horizons', in *Sunda and Sahul. Prehistoric Studies in Southeast Asia. Melanesia and Australia,* Allen, J., Golson, J. & Jones, R. (eds.) Academic Press, London. A discussion of the development of Motu trading systems, relevant both theoretically and comparatively for an evaluation of the kula trade.

546. Austen, L. (1939) 'Megalithic Structures in the Trobriand Islands', in *Oceania,* Vol x, pp. 30–53. A descriptive article containing diagrams and photographs of structures. Austen's speculations are relevant to the arguments concerning rank in the Trobriands.

547. Churchill, William (1916) *Sissano: Movements of Migration Within and Through Melanesia.* Carnegie Institute of Washington, Publication No. 244, Washington. Of minor relevance, concerned with initial migration and inter-island contact, argued mainly from linguistic evidence. The maps of hypothetical migration are of some importance to compare with conjectures about trade routes and long sea voyaging put forth on the basis of archaeological evidence.

548. Crosby, Eleanor (1973) 'A Comparative Study of Melanesian Hafted Edgetools and other Percussive Cutting Implements'. Unpublished Ph.D. Thesis, ANU, Canberra. On Woodlark tool materials.

549. Damon, F.H. (1978?) 'On the Dead Hands of the Ancestors: Megalithic Structures on Woodlark Island'. Unpublished. Discussion of megalithic structures and trenches highlighting their relationship to current ideology and contrasting them to their Trobriand analogues.

550. Earle, Timothy K. & Ericson, J.E. (eds.) (1977) *Exchange Systems in Prehistory.* Academic Press, London. See also Dalton, G. (1977) (item 210) and Gall, Patricia et al. (1977) (item 252).

551. Egloff, B.J. (1971) 'Collingwood Bay and the Trobriand Islands in Recent Prehistory'. Unpublished Ph.D. Thesis, ANU, Canberra.

552. Egloff, B.J. (1972) 'The Sepulchral Pottery of Nuamata Island, Papua', in

Archaeology and Physical Anthropology in Oceania, Vol. VII, No. 2, July, 1972. The article provides a new perspective on prehistoric exchange and trade in coastal and inland Papua. Section on the ceramic trade suggests that the kula 'could be considered as resulting from an overdevelopment of normal trade' where the institution of trade partnership is crucial.

553. Egloff, B.J. (1977) *Pottery of Papua New Guinea: the National Collection*. National Arts School of Papua New Guinea for the Trustees of the PNG National Museum and Art Gallery, Port Moresby, May, 1977, pp. 5-7, 10, 16-25, 93. Photographs and drawings and locational maps of pottery making of Mailu, Collingwood Bay, Engineer Group, Brooker, East Cape, Goodenough and Amphletts. Brief text on attitudes to pottery making and on the social significance of pots.

554. Egloff, B.J. (1978) 'The Kula before Malinowski: a changing configuration', in *Mankind*, 11:3, pp. 429-435. On the archaeological evidence of changes in the pottery trade, Egloff argues that the kula probably extended to the Collingwood Bay area in recent prehistoric period.

555. Forth, R.L. (1965) 'Stone Arrangements on Woodlark Island', in *Mankind*, Vol. 6 (6), November. A descriptive article noting the similarity between structures on Murua (Woodlark Island) and the Trobriands.

556. Gerrits, G.J.M. (1974) 'Burial canoes and canoe-burials in the Trobriand and Marshall Bennett Islands (Melanesia)', in *Anthropos*, Vol. 69, pp. 224-231. An archaeological discussion of the remains of canoe burials on Kitava, Iwa and Woodlark Island. Mentions recent changes in the type of ordinary sea-going canoes.

557. Heers, G. (1971) See Holdsworth, D.K. (1971) item 561.

558. Heers, G. (1970, 1972, 1973) See Ollier, C.D. (1970, 1972, 1973) items 574-576.

559. Hodder, I. (1975) 'Regression analysis of some trade and marketing patterns', in *World Archaeology*, 6, pp. 172-189. No mention of kula. British archaeology. 'Artefact distributions are studied as measures of contact or interaction with a production, marketing or service centre.' This article presents a way of deducing trade patterns from archaeological evidence and as such is relevant to current studies of kula.

560. Holdsworth, D.K. (1968, 1970, 1972, 1973) See Ollier, C.D. (1968, 1970, 1972, 1973) items 572-576.

561. Holdsworth, D.K. & Heers, G. (1971) 'Some Medicinal and Poisonous Plants from the Trobriand Islands, Milne Bay District', in *Records of the Papua and New Guinea Public Museum and Art Gallery*, Vol. 1, No. 2. The article links common medicinal practice through Kula Ring area to contact through kula.

562. Holdsworth, D.K. & Ollier, C.D. (1973) 'Magic Stones and Megaliths of the Trobriand Islands, Papua, New Guinea', in *Occasional Papers of the Anth-*

ropology Museum, University of Queensland, No. 2, 1973, p. 135. This
paper argues that the megaliths were funerary monuments of leading men.
It is relevant in that the material evidence of cultural similarity can be the
basis for discussing trade routes and their historical transformation.

563. Hughes, Ian (1973) 'Stone-age trade in the New Guinea island: a historical
geography without history', in *The Pacific in Transition*, Brookfield,
Harold (ed.) ANU Press, Canberra, p. 122. (see item 171).

564. Irwin, G.J. (1978) 'Pots and entrepôts: a study of settlement, trade and
the development of economic specialization in Papuan prehistory', in
World Archaeology, Vol. 9, No. 3, February, 1978. Discusses the emergence of Mailu as a central trading community and producer of pottery for
trade. An important contribution in terms of theoretical and historical
interpretation of primitive and pre-historic trade in the Massim.

565. Irwin, G. See also entry in Anthropological material section, item 309.

566. Lauer, P.K. (1970) 'Pottery Traditions in the D'Entrecasteaux Islands of
Papua' Ph.D. Thesis, ANU, Canberra. See also Lauer, P.K. (1974) (item
569).

567. Lauer, P.K. (1971) 'Changing Patterns of Pottery Trade in the Trobriand
Islands', in *World Archaeology*, 3, pp. 197-209. Discusses the decline of
the pottery trade and changes in the kula over pre-historic and colonial
period. Lauer includes a map indicating centres of pottery importation
on the Trobriands. He suggests that there has been 'a loosening of the
kula trade nexus with the arrival of Europeans', and gives evidence of
extensive inter-island trade going back over centuries.

568. Lauer, P.K. (1973) 'Miadeba Pottery', in *Records of the Papua New
Guinea Public Museum and Art Gallery*, No. 3, 1973. Refers to distribution of pottery throughout Massim as following kula patterns.

569. Lauer, P.K. (1974) 'Pottery Traditions in the D'Entrecasteaux Islands of
Papua', in *Occasional Papers in Anthropology*, No. 3, University of Queensland. The introduction by K.P. Koepping discusses the relationship between the new archaeology and anthropological approches to the study
of trade. The text is substantially the same as Lauer's Ph.D. thesis and
contains analyses of production and technology of pottery, ethnographic
variations within the D'Entrecasteaux and a considerable amount of
information on prehistoric pottery production and inter-island trade. In
terms of a radical intervention into the debate on the meaning and functions of the kula, Lauer's conclusions on the 'Emerging Pictures of Past
Pottery Trade' constitute a major contribution.

570. Lyons, A.P. (1922) 'Sepulchral pottery of Murua, Papua', in *MAN*,
93. Of minor importance.

571. Mackay, Roy D. (1971) 'An Historic Engraved Shell from the Trobriand
Islands-Milne Bay District', in *Records of the Papua & New Guinea Public*

Museums and Art Gallery, Vol. 1, No. 1, April. The shell is identified as an early *mwali* and linked with another shell in Australian Museum, Sydney.

572. Ollier, C.D. & Holdsworth, D.K. (1968) 'A Survey of a Megalithic Structure in the Trobriand Islands, Papua', in *Archaeology and Physical Anthropology in Oceania*, III, (2), pp. 156–158. Of minor importance as an isolated item but forms part of a body of archaeological literature relevant to inter-island contact. See also Ollier, C.D., Holdsworth, D.K. & Heers, G. (1972, 1973) (items 575–576).

573. Ollier, C.D. & Holdsworth, D.K. (1968) 'Caves of Kiriwina, Trobriand Islands, Papua', in *Helictite*, 6, (4), July. Of minor importance.

574. Ollier, C.D., Holdsworth, D.K. & Heers, G. (1970) 'Megaliths of Kitava, Trobriand Islands', in *Records of the Papua New Guinea Museum*, 1, pp. 5–15. See also Ollier, C.D. & Holdsworth, D.K. (1968)

575. Ollier, C.D., Holdsworth, D.K. & Heers, G. (1972) 'Stone Structures of Tuma and Kaileuna, Trobriand Islands', in *Archaeology and Physical Anthropology in Oceania*, VII, (1), pp. 41–50. See also Ollier, C.D. & Holdsworth, D.K. (1968) (item 572) p. 51. Offerings to spirits on Tuma.

576. Ollier, C.D., Holdsworth, D.K. & Heers, G. (1973) 'Megaliths, Stones and Bwala on Kitava, Trobriand Islands, Papua', in *Archaeology and Physical Anthropology in Oceania*, VIII (1), pp. 41–50. See also Ollier, C.D., & Holdsworth, D.K. (1968) (items 572, 573).

577. Ollier, C.D. (1973) See Holdsworth, D.K. (1973) item 562.

578. Parker, R.S. (1971) See Epstein, A.L. (1971) item 225.

579. Shutler, Richard Jnr. & Mary Elizabeth (1975) *Oceanic Prehistory*. Cummings, Menlo Park, California, p. 56. Textbook. Draws attention to the relative lack of archaeological research in the Massim and to Egloff's work which presents large trade networks as being at least 1,000 years old.

580. Smith, I.E. (1974) 'Obsidian Sources in Papua-New Guinea', in *Archaeology and Physical Anthropology in Oceania*, Vol. IX, No. 1, pp. 18–25. The article is mainly technical, on the chemical composition of obsidian, but the distinction between Eastern and Western Fergusson deposits is important in discerning trade contact from archaeological remains.

581. Williams, F.E. (1936) 'Report on Stone Structures in the Trobriands – Little Stonehenge', in *Pacific Islands Monthly*, June, 1936. A very brief reference; for a more anthropological report see Austen, L. (1939 and 1940) (items 546, 133).

Massim Art and Aesthetics of Kula Objects

582. Barrow, T. (1962) See Bühler, A. (1962) item 588.
583. Bartlett, H.K. (1937) See Tindale, N.B. (1937) item 616.
584. Beier, Ulli (1975) 'Aesthetic Concepts in the Trobriand Islands', in *Gibibori*, Vol. 2, No. 1, April. Institute of Papua New Guinea Studies and Niugini Press, pp. 36–39. Principally about the aesthetics and semantics of carving with special reference to canoe prow boards. Kula canoes stated as the most valuable kind of carving, even above yamhouses (p. 39).
585. Beier, U. (1978) 'The Mwali Shell as Art Object and Status Symbol', in *Oral History*, Vol. VI, No. 3, pp. 78–86.
586. British Museum (1906) 'An Illustrated Register of the Cooke-Daniels Expedition Collection'. Ethnological Documents 1010. Unpublished B.M. papers, pp. 124–183 and unnumbered pages.
587. British Museum (1922) 'An Illustrated Register of the Bronislaw Malinowski Collection'. 42 pages, including Ethnological Documents 1009, pages unnumbered. Unpublished B.M. papers, London.
588. Bühler, A., Barrow, T. & Mountford, C.P. (1962) *Oceania & Australia – The Art of the South Seas.* London. General discussion of art forms over whole area. Good illustrations.
589. Dark, Phillip J. (1975) 'A Note on Collections', in *Pacific Art Newsletter (PAN)*, No. 2, December, 1975, p. 5. Mentions the creation of a large Trobriand Collection at the Papua New Guinea Museum, including kula ornaments.
590. Dickson, T. Elder & Whitehouse, E. (1943) 'Ceremonial Lime Spatulae from British New Guinea', in *MAN*, Vol. XLII, No. 29, pp. 49–51. Discussion of a two-pronged spatula considered exceptionally valuable in the kula. Found at Louisiades, made on Tagula or Misima. 'Held by women dancing', 'owned by married women'. Illustrated.
591. Dickson, T. Elder (1946) See Seligmann, C.G. (1946) item 615.

592. Ellis, Silas (1924) 'Art of the Trobriand Islander', in *The Studio*, Vol. 88. London Offices of the Studio, London, pp. 132-135.

593. Graburn, N.H.H. (1977) 'Contemporary Problems in the Art of Oceania', (Report of Workshop 1), in *Pacific Art Newsletter (PAN)*, No. 5, June, 1977, pp. 3-10. Report of a discussion which includes comments about the contemporary production of carvings for the kula trade.

594. Haddon, Alfred C. (1893-1894) 'Wood-carving in the Trobriands', in *Illustrated Archaelogist*, Vol. 1, pp. 107-112.

595. Haddon, A.C. (1894) *The Decorative Art of British New Guinea: A Study in Papuan Ethnography*. (With 12 plates, map and numerous woodcuts). The Academy House, University Press, Dublin, pp. 184-245 n.b. 203, 223, 225, 233, 238. Although mainly concerned with descriptions of artefacts and designs on them, there is some information on production and trade of these items. Mentions Woodlark Island trade with Teste Island for pottery, the display of stone axe blades and the construction of canoes on Panaeati. There are some misunderstandings and his observations on the 'influence of Trobriand art style' throughout the area might actually be evidence of the trade in carved objects rather than cultural imitation. This study contains an excellent bibliography of almost all nineteenth-century published material which contained any ethnographic references to the Massim. Almost all Haddon's references are to first-hand observations. Copiously illustrated.

596. Haddon, Alfred C. (1895) *Evolution in Art*. Walter Scott Ltd., London, pp. 47, 58, 224, 228. Pre-Malinowski. Haddon attempts to construct an anthropological approach to the study of art and design. Involves a general discussion of the translation of natural form into artistic form: its variety and purpose. Mentions Massim trade in artistic objects, differences in form and style and shell artefacts as money and specific medium of exchange.

597. Haddon, A.C. (1912) *Arts and Crafts, in Reports on the Cambridge Anthropological Expedition to Torres Straits*, Vol. IV. C.U.P., London.

598. Hooper, James T. (1943) 'Another Lime Spatula from New Guinea, and a Turtleshell Comb', in *MAN*, No. 81, pp. 95-96. Correspondence arising from T. Elder Dickson's article (item 590) describes spatula and comb from Louisiade Island.

599. Krieger, Herbert W. (1932) 'Design areas in Oceania', in *Proceedings of the United States National Museum*, Vol. 79, Art. 30. Washington D.C. Not seen by editor.

600. Lewis, Albert Buell (1973) *Decorative Art of New Guinea*. Republication of 2 booklets originally published by the Field Museum, Chicago. 1. *Incised Designs*. 2. *Carved and Painted Designs*. Dover, N.Y. Contains photographs of carved lime spatulae, canoe ornaments, etc. and details processes of production. No mention of trade. Marginal.

601. Lindblom, G. (1943) 'Crescent Shaped Lime Spatulas from British New Guinea', in *MAN*, No. 119, p. 143. Correspondence arising from T. Elder Dickson's article (item 590) suggesting that the object is used as a pestle for crushing betel-nuts in other areas. These items are important valuables on islands of the Southern Massim.
602. Linton, Ralph & Wingert, Paul S. (1946) *Arts of the South Seas*. The museum of Modern Art. Simon & Schuster, N.Y., pp. 141-150. The art of the Massim, emphasis on the Trobriands. Maintains that the art style is 'nearly homogeneous'. Photographs.
603. Mountford, C.P. (1962) See Bühler, A. (1962) item 588.
604. Munn, Nancy (1971) *The Symbolism of Perceptual Qualities: A Study in Trobriand Ritual Aesthetics*. Paper delivered at American Anthropological Association.
605. Narubutal (Narubutau), Chief (1975) 'Trobriand Canoe Prows: Fourteen Pieces from the National Collection in the Papua New Guinea Museum', in *Gibibori*, Vol. 2, No. 1, April. Institute of Papua New Guinea Studies and Niugini Press, pp. 1-14. Indigenous information and interpretation about motifs in the carved canoe prows of sailing canoes. Author is leader of Yalumgwa village and a recognized master carver.
606. Newton, Douglas (1975) *Massim, Art of the Massim Area, New Guinea*. The Museum of Primitive Art, New York, pp. 2-9 general, pp. 10-19 canoes and trade. The text contains a useful summary of the kula and the various ways in which art styles reveal and reflect trade systems. Excellent illustrations and bibliography.
607. Norick, Frank Albert (1976) 'An Analysis of the Material Culture of the Trobriand Islands based upon the Collection of Bronislaw Malinowski'. Dissertation for Ph.D. University of California, Berkeley.
608. Outram, Catherine (1974) 'Massim Art'. Honours Thesis, Art Department, University of Hawaii. Cited by Norick, F.A. (item 607).
609. Pfund, Kurt (1972) *Islands of Love: Portrait of the Trobriand Islands*. Rigby, Adelaide. Marginal. Paintings of kula objects.
610. Scoditti, Giancarlo (1975) 'Aesthetic Space and Artist in an Ethnological Society'. Unpublished paper presented at a Symposium - 'Art, Artisans & Society', University of Leicester, Department of Architecture, Leicester, January, 1975.
611. Scoditti, Giancarlo (1977) 'A Kula Prowboard - An Iconological Interpretation', in *L'Uomo*, Vol. 1, No. 2, pp. 199-232. Attempts to explain the probable visual meaning of the carved prowboard of a Kitavan kula canoe, involving an iconological interpretation relating the engraved symbols to their verbal meanings. Contains illustrations and diagrams.
612. Scoditti, Giancarlo (1978) 'The Use of the Computer in the Formal Interpretation of the Kula Canoes' Prowboards'. Paper presented to the first

Int. Congress on Automatic Processing of Art-History Data and Documents. Scuola Normale Superiore, Pisa, 1978.

613. Scoditti, Giancarlo (in press) *Ethnographicus Kitavensis: Iconology and Semantics*, Vol. 1, Rome.

614. Seligmann, C.G. (1909) 'A Type of Canoe Ornament with Magical Significance for Southeastern New Guinea', in *MAN*, 16, pp. 33-35. Mainly concerned with remarking the design and 'magical' nature of canoe ornaments. Mentions story of an administrator encountering 3-4 decorated canoes from Murua at Misima. Mentions a village called Modan on Murua noted for canoe manufacture and carving.

615. Seligmann, C.G. & Dickson, T. Elder (1946) ' "Rajim" and "tabuya" of the d'Entrecasteaux group', in *MAN*, 46, article 112, pp. 129-134. On the designs on canoes, particularly a motif of a man, a 'culture-hero'. Only remotely connected, but of interest to compare with N. Munn's and G. Scoditti's work.

616. Tindale, N.B. & Bartlett, H.K. (1937) 'Notes on Some Clay Pots from Paneaeti Islands, Southeast of New Guinea', in *Transactions of the Royal Society of South Australia*, Vol. LXI. Details of ceremonial pots: made on the island by women, claim to be able to tell individual maker even if found in a 'foreign land' or years later. Pots exchanged for sago with Misima, Kimuta, Ware, Tubetube, Calvados Island as far as Sudest. Methodist mission (1928) appears to have brought pots to Rossel Island.

617. Whitehouse, E. (1943) See Dickson, T. Elder (1943) item 590.

618. Wingert, P.S. (1946) See Linton, R. (1946) item 602.

Films

619. Cook, Boris (1967) *Legend in Clay*. 16mm colour sound ethnographic film. Ten minutes. Office of Information of Government of Papua New Guinea. Also distributed by Royal Anthropological Institute Film Library. Technology and making of clay pots in the Amphlett Islands.
620. Ichioka, Yasuko (1972) *Kula: Argonauts of the Western Pacific*. 16mm colour sound ethnographic documentary shot 1970–1971. NAV Productions, Tokyo. 62 minutes. BBC-TV version 1973, *Kula: a Reason for Giving*. Full-length documentary on kula sailing from Sinaketa in Trobriands to Amphletts to Fergusson and to Normanby. Shows fleet of nine canoes, some rented for film. Shows sailing, kula hospitality, kula conversations, acquisition of necklaces, problems of kula timing. Important interview material with Tokavataria, senior leader of Sinaketa. Names many necklaces.
621. Leach, Jerry W. (1975) *Trobriand Cricket: an Ingenious Response to Colonialism*. 16mm documentary produced by Office of Information of Papua New Guinea Government. Distributed by Royal Anthropological Institute, Concord Films Council and University of California Extension Media Center.
622. Nisbett, Alec (1975) *The Trobriand Experiment*. BBC-TV Horizon documentary. Not distributed. 62 minutes. Fragments of information on kula and sailing in 1975 in opening sequence.
623. Powell, Harry A. (1951) *The Trobriand Islanders*. 16mm colour sound ethnographic film. 67 minutes. Distributed by Royal Anthropological Institute Film Library. One section on sail-making and canoe preparation for 1951 kula voyage from northern Kiriwina to Kitava. Principally about preparations for kula. Kula section is the third of a four-part film.
624. Szabo, Steve (1967) *The Kula*. 16mm colour sound documentary. 25 minutes. Office of Information of Government of Papua New Guinea. Also distributed by Royal Anthropological Institute Film Library. Shows making of armshells in Trobriands (staged). Shows inland kula of the

simultaneous type in northern Kiriwina. Poor material on kula discussions. Magic used is not kula magic. Shows trawler voyage to south Kiriwina and canoe voyage to Vakuta and the Amphletts. A small expedition. Filmed route probably created by subjects for the sake of the film as it is very aberrant.

625. Villeminot, J. (1967) *Les Seigneurs des mers du sud*. Ethnographic film. Connaissance du Monde, Paris. Film of daily life in Trobriands.

Museum Collections

There are numerous substantial collections of Massim material culture. The German ethnologist Otto Finsch compiled the first major collection of artefacts in the 1880s, most of which were deposited in the museums at Brunswick (Braunschweig) and Vienna, although a few pieces exist in the Pitt-Rivers Museum and other European museums. From this period to the present day, we have at least one substantial collection for each decade of European contact.

Most of the major collections were amassed between the years 1890 and 1919. The collections of P. Black (Buffalo), Rev. Fellows (Canberra) and William MacGregor (Queensland, Aberdeen and Cambridge) were made with the express purpose of having comprehensive and documented records of the native culture of the Massim. Seligmann, on the Cooke-Daniels expedition in 1908, also aimed at producing a systematic record of all items *traded* in the area. In view of this intention and his large collection of kula objects of all types, it was interesting to see that his own ethnographic notes which accompany the Cooke-Daniels Collection in the British Museum list the *mwali* in order of value. He refers to those items made of *Conus* shells as *kulatana* which he took to be the native name for the shell. It is not, and the only meaning for this term that has been suggested is it is made up of 'kula' and 'tana' meaning 'one'. So perhaps Seligmann did have an informant who provided him with a description of the kula in terms of the different values of armshells, but lacking familiarity with the language he misinterpreted this reference. Museum documentation often contains such errors: there are at least two necklaces attributed to 'the *Bagi* tribe' in British collections and it is clear from some notes that the collector has assumed that the decorations on armshells and necklaces are the valued objects. Indeed, one can only admire the Massim trader who managed to convince a traveller that the helmet shell and pandanus ornament on a *bagi* were the desirable objects and so gained doubly on the exchange! (An example is the *bagi* in the American Museum of Natural History.) Although museum ethnographic notes are rarely extensive or even reliable, sometimes they provide new information and often they confirm ethnographic information in records and other documents.

Even when information is scant or unreliable in specific terms, the collections themselves often reveal significant information about exchange. For example, there is evidence for inflation in the kula trade as pacification occurs, when the armshells gradually stop circulating in pairs. There are no pairs of armshells collected in the northern area after 1896, but in the Southern Massim Seligmann collected several pairs of *mwali* as late as 1908. More interestingly, there are very few *bagi* outside Papua New Guinea at all, and at no time did Massim traders part readily with fine quality *bagi*. The only museum examples which, according to the standards of evaluation described by Malinowski (item 7) and Campbell (item 181), would be classified as of high quality are held by the Papua New Guinea Museum and Art Gallery. In Malinowski's notes to the British Museum Collection he refers to the *bagi* or *soulava* necklace as 'the *real* kula valuable'; their comparative value and rarity in the Massim is borne out by their absence from otherwise comprehensive collections of ornaments.

The distribution of items, the variations which are discernible in terms of style, date of collection and provenance pose many problems for research. Some items, such as the *sapi-sapi* belts and the *soulava* necklaces are rare and, when provenanced, seem to have been acquired mainly from the South. Others, such as *Conus* armshells and boar's tusk necklaces, are relatively common and often come from the D'Entrecasteaux Islands. The *doga* (or *dona*) in collections usually appear well-worn, the sheen and colour suggesting long usage. Many of the armshells, however, seem to be 'straight off the production line', their surfaces are white and slightly chalky and they show no signs of having been decorated with seeds, beads or pandanus streamers. A systematic study of collections could illuminate many aspects of colonial intervention in native trading systems and the changing values of particular items. Many kula items in museums are described as insignia of rank. This may be a misrepresentation of their meaning, but it is suggestive of the increasing democratization of kula which has been noted by anthropologists.

The museum collections are valuable sources of information and provide confirmation of trade throughout the Massim; they also contain an historical record of the technology and the aesthetics of Massim society for the past century. As yet there have been no comprehensive studies of Massim material culture which situate trade, technology, manufacture and aesthetics in anthropological or historical perspective. This brief summary of museums is presented as a stimulus to such research.

Australia

Canberra, A.C.T. *Australian National Gallery*. There are many items from the Massim area but the outstanding collection is that made by the Rev. Fellows in the late nineteenth century, purchased by the Australian Government in 1973. Fellows' diaries are held with the collection, which is at present in storage.

Canberra, A.C.T. *National Ethnographic Collection, Institute of Anatomy, Department of Health.* There are several items of interest, a number of fine *doga* and ornaments using sapi-sapi.

Sydney, N.S.W. *The Australian Museum.* This is one of the largest collections of Massim artefacts, totalling approximately 2,500 items and including examples of all valuables traded in the kula.

St. Lucia, Queensland. *Anthropology Museum, University of Queensland.* The museum has a collection of Trobriand material culture items collected around 1950 by a Mr. Healy — trading items such as mortars and pestles, lime containers and spatulae and wooden bowls and clay pots form the collection, which has some excellent items. Dr. Peter Lauer, the curator, has also made a collection of Massim pottery, some types of which constitute vaygua in the kula (see item 569).

Brisbane, Queensland. *Queensland Museum.* This museum has one of the most substantial Massim collections in the world and there are many kula items. Of major interest is the MacGregor Collection, made by officers of the British New Guinea Government under Sir William MacGregor's administration between 1889 and 1898. There are about 45 *mwali*, some in pairs, some still decorated with beads and pandanus, 75 axe blades (about half of these were probably 'ceremonial') 445 lime spatulae and six pottery bowls used for feasts and classified as 'valuables'. There are also many other examples of artefacts traded in the context of the kula.

Adelaide, South Australia. *South Australian Museum.*

Melbourne, Victoria. *National Museum of Victoria.* There are over a thousand artefacts from the Massim, most of these in two Trobriand Island Collections. The first was made by Malinowski in 1919 and is similar to the British Museum Collection. The Page Collection was purchased in 1974 and contains many items traded in the context of the kula and a particularly fine example of a *bagi*. There is another *bagi* collected in the Southern Massim about 1901; it is highly decorated with trade store beads. There are notes made by Malinowski on Trobriand material culture and 33 photographs; the notes are copies of those in the British Museum and most of the photographs have been published.

Perth, Western Australia. *The State Museum.* Ethnological Collections. No information available.

Hobart, Tasmania. *Tasmanian Museum and Art Gallery.* Most Massim items collected between 1898 and 1918 with one early lime spatula brought back in 1831; 11 *mwali*; 3 axe blades and 52 lime spatulae.

The Kula: a bibliography

Canada

Toronto. *Royal Ontario Museum.*

Ottawa. *National Museum of Man.* A small collection of New Guinea material which includes a few axe blades and lime spatulae collected in the early 1960s by a Miss Vellacott-Jones.

Europe

Denmark

Copenhagen. *National Museum of Denmark.* One Trobriand *mwali,* acquired in 1959, offered as one of a pair.

France

Paris. *Musée de l'Homme.* There is a collection of Massim items which includes at least one *bagi* and one *mwali.*

Holland

Leiden. *Rijksmuseum voor Volkenkunde*

Bergen op Zoom. Dr Gerrits (Private Collection).

Amsterdam. *Koninklijk Instituut voor de Tropen.*

Hungary

Budapest. *Ethnographical Museum.* Geza Roheim Collection of 211 pieces from East Normanby made in 1930 and an earlier collection of 220 items made between 1910 and 1920 by a trader, K. Verebélyi.

Italy

Rome. *Museo Preistorico ed Etnografico L. Pigorini.*

Switzerland

Basle. *Museum für Völkerkunde.* A major collection of Massim artefacts.

West Germany

Berlin. *Museum Für Völkerkunde.*

Braunschweig (Brunswick). *Museum für Völkerkunde.* Otto Finsch Collection, made in the nineteenth century.

Göttingen. *Museum, Institut für Völkerkunde an der Universität Göttinghan.* A substantial collection of Massim artefacts made by Professor E. Schlesier during the period 1961/1962, it includes about 100 kula items.

Hamburg. *Hamburgisches Museum für Völkerkunde und Vorgeschichte.*

New Zealand

Wellington. *National Museum of New Zealand.* There are five *Mwali,* two sapi-sapi ornaments, five lime spatulae, eight adze blades and one hafted blade and five hafts of the type illustrated in Seligmann (see item 481), plate LXI. Most of these items were collected in the nineteenth century.

Dunedin. *Otago Museum.* Although mostly unprovenanced, the items are definitely from the Massim. There are 17 *mwali,* two *bagi,* 168 lime spatulae, including two of whalebone and about twenty axe blades.

Papau New Guinea

Boroko. *Papau New Guinea National Museum and Art Gallery.* There are twenty-two kula items in the museum; some of them are highly valued in exchange, indeed one *doga* is classified as priceless. There are three *bagi,* three *mwali,* six ceremonial axe heads and a variety of other ornaments, most originating in the Trobriand Islands.

United Kingdon

Aberdeen, Scotland. *Anthropological Museum, Marischal College, University of Aberdeen.* This museum holds part of the large collection made by Sir William MacGregor; includes seven ceremonial axes and over 116 lime spatulae from the Massim.

Birmingham, England. *City of Birmingham Museum and Art Gallery.* The collection of Massim material consists of twenty-four lime spatulae and seven *mwali.* Most items were collected by a Birmingham man between 1889 and 1920.

Cambridge, England. *Museum of Archaeology and Anthropology, University of Cambridge.* The museum has a large collection of Massim material, most of it collected prior to 1902. There are more than twenty *mwali,* one an exceptionally fine kula object showing the ivory-like striations and patina associated with age and handling. There are two short sapi-sapi necklets and twelve *doga.* There are several pots and carved dishes of the type used in trade and many lime spatulae, including some made of bone, which may have been kula valuables. Many of these items were collected by anthropologists.

Edinburgh, Scotland. *The Royal Scottish Museum.* There are seven *mwali,* two constitute a 'pair' and were collected before 1883. Six sapi-sapi necklaces, all but one collected in the late nineteenth century, and eight ceremonial axe blades. There is a piece of pottery from Ware in the Southern Massim.

Glasgow, Scotland. *Hunterian Museum, The University.* Two *mwali* and four lime spatulae, all collected prior to 1877.

Hastings, England. *Hastings Museum and Art Gallery.* Two *mwali*, about a dozen lime spatulae and several axe blades, all collected by Lord and Lady Brassey in either 1876 or 1887.

Liverpool, England. *Merseyside County Museum.* There are twenty-six *mwali*, about forty-five axe blades (only some ceremonial), about seventy lime spatulae and one *bagi* which is the earliest example encountered, having been collected before 1851 by a Captain T.H. Foster. Apart from the Foster material, most other items were collected by missionaries in New Guinea about the turn of the century.

London, England. *London School of Economics,* Anthropological Collection.

London, England. *British Museum.* This is probably the most extensive and comprehensive collection of Massim material culture, comprising the Cooke Daniels Expedition Collection which was made by Seligmann and the Robert Mond Collection made by Malinowski, as well as numerous smaller collections made by seamen, missionaries and other anthropologists. Most of Malinowski's material was made on the Trobriand Islands and Seligmann's collection was made in the Southern Massim, mainly on Tubetube. There are useful notes on the objects for both collections and rare items such as a fine quality *bagi*, several whalebone spatulae, egg cowrie ornaments, and sapi-sapi belts, many of which were classified as valuables which could be traded in the kula. Both Malinowski and Seligmann collected a range of axe and adze blades and there are several very large *beku* from Suloga. There are hundreds of carved lime spatulae from the area and a few lime gourds of the type used by 'guyaus' or leaders which are profusely decorated with sapi-sapi, pearl shell and banana seeds and make the clinking sound of the other *vaygua* traded in the kula.

Newcastle upon Tyne, England. *The Hancock Museum.* The George Brown Collection of Massim artefacts is reputedly large and contains exceptionally high quality items.

Oxford, England. *Pitt-Rivers Museum, Department of Ethnology and Prehistory, University of Oxford.* The earliest material was donated by retired seamen, recent material coming from missionaries anthropologists and visitors. The material collected by Jenness is of great interest and includes a set of six armshells (moali) showing the manufacturing process. The earliest *mwali*, collected by Otto Finsch in the late 1880s from the D'Entrecasteaux area uses slightly more of the shell than is usual but is otherwise similar in style and decoration. The Pitt-Rivers Collection of shell armlets spans the colonial period and is useful in establishing variations in manufacture and ornamentation as there are items from several islands of the Massim. There are at least twenty-four *doga* (or *dona*) boar's tusk necklaces and twelve necklaces made from pink *Spondylus* or *Chama pacifica* as the museum was in the process of moving parts of the collection, I was unable to see these and so could only identify one as a *bagi*. There were at least 200 axe or adze blades from the Massim, most cited as coming from Suloga or Woodlark. They were collected by Codrington, Seligmann, and Jenness. Other interesting items include a card of glass and porcelain beads made for the Melanesian market and the superb collection of photographic plates taken by Jenness (see item 59).

Plymouth, England. *City of Plymouth, Museum & Art Gallery.* This collection is particularly interesting, consisting largely of items collected by the Rev. H.M. Dauncey, a missionary in the 1880s. Several other museums have pieces from this collection but the major part went to Plymouth. There are four *mwali*, five necklaces made from sapi-sapi, one appears to be similar to a *bagi* in the British Museum Collection which has a baler shell ornament instead of the more usual helmet shell, the others are probably *doga* with the 'tusk' being made of the base of a *Conus* shell. There are twenty-five lime spatulae and ten axes which may be *beku*, six are termed 'ceremonial'.

Sheffield, England. *City of Sheffield Museum.* Three striated axe/adze blades which may be of Massim origin.

Whitby, England. *Whitby Museum.* This small museum contains many items brought to Whitby by seamen and other travellers. Its collection includes a necklace collected around 1880 and described as 'Shells used as money' which may be part of a *bagi*.

United States of America

Berkeley, California. *Lowie Museum of Anthropology.* The Malinowski Collection here compares well with those held in London and Melbourne but the kula objects are not so fine in quality. The Principal Museum Anthropologist, Dr. Frank Norick has produced a major study of the collection. Recently the museum acquired some Trobriand artefacts collected by Dr. Annette Weiner.

Honolulu, Hawaii. *Bernice P. Bishop Museum.* A small collection, mostly collected at the turn of the century. One definitely identified *mwali* from Normanby Island and a number of other *Conus* shell armbands, ten lime spatulae.

Honolulu, Hawaii. *Honolulu Academy of Arts.* A collection of Massim art, no details available.

Chicago, Illinois. *Field Museum of Natural History.*

Baltimore, Maryland. *The Museum of Art.*

Cambridge, Mass. *Peabody Museum, Harvard University.* There are two important nineteenth century collections. The first was made by A.P. Goodwin about 1888. Brief notes indicate that Goodwin was aware of the ceremonial use and high value placed on a variety of traded items. All the *mwali* he collected are in pairs and he noted 'Armbands of all sizes are used as currency in the Massim'. The green striated axe blades originating from Suloga were not used; however, the adzes were used as tools. The other collection, made in 1896 by one Alexanderer Agasiz, contains a model of a canoe made in the Marshall Bennetts, a wide range of shell ornaments, lime spatulae, mortars and pestles. The carvings are very fine and the whole collection is of great historical importance. Interestingly there are no *bagi* in either of the old collections nor in the smaller, more recent ones.

Newark, New Jersey. *Newark Museum.*

Buffalo, New York. *Buffalo Museum of Science.* The museum holds a substantial Papua-New Guinea collection made by P.G. Black who worked for Burns Philp Trading Co. in the area during the period 1886-1916. It contains seventeen *mwali* from the D'Entrecasteaux area and 225 Trobriand lime spatulae as well as a couple of pieces of pottery from the kula area.

New York. *The American Museum of Natural History.* Two *bagi*, one recently collected from Jinju, Rossel Island. The other is of interest as it contains wooden sections and seems to have been acquired for the helmet shell ornament. Three *mwali*, one collected around 1904. Seven striated axe blades from the Massim area collected before 1881. Sixty lime spatulae collected during early colonial period.

Philadelphia. *University Museum of Pennsylvania.*

Union of Soviet Socialist Republics

Leningrad. *State Museum, Ethnological Department.*

Appendix

A Note on Shells and Kula Valuables

Since the publication of *Argonauts of the Western Pacific* everybody has known that two kinds of shell ornaments circulate in the kula – red necklaces made out of *Spondylus* and white armshells made out of *Conus millepunctatus*.

But it is really not that simple.

Strings of red shell discs have a wide distribution in Micronesia and Melanesia. Two genera have mainly been mentioned in the literature as material for such discs – *Spondylus* (thorny oysters) and *Chama* (jewel boxes). Both live attached to coral rocks in more or less the same habitat. But zoologically they are widely different genera, belonging to two different subclasses of the class Bivalvia.

Malinowski mentions three areas of origin of kula necklaces. The fine *vaygua* (*or soulava*) necklaces came from two sources. One was the area around Port Moresby. Another 'the islands of Sud-Est, Rossel, and the surrounding small islands (1922: pp. 506–507). The coarser necklaces of the *katudababile* type were made in the southern Trobriands out of *kaloma* shells fished in the Sanaroa Lagoon east of Fergusson Island. (*ibid.* pp. 358, 367ff.) According to Malinowski they are all *Spondylus*.

Doing fieldwork in Rossel (Yela) in 1973 I collected specimens of the shells still used to make the indigenous 'shell-money' – the *ndap* and *ko* – and red shell necklaces. The shells were identified by Dr. Jorgen Knudsen of the Zoological Museum of the University of Copenhagen, to whom I am also grateful for additional information on Pacific shells. The Rossel *ndap* are made from various species of *Spondylus*, while the *ko*, and the shell discs, are made from a *Chama* species (*C. (pacifica) imbricata* Broderip).

This came as a surprise to me. I therefore consulted Malinowski again. His description of the *kaloma* – 'a shell, the size and shape of a hollowed out half of a pear, and of a flat, small lid' (*ibid.* p. 371), and the shell seen in the picture plate L(A), matched with the *Chama* I collected at Rossel. The *Spondylus* has a much less convex shell. Moreover Seligmann supposed the Massim necklaces to be from *Chama* (1910: p. 514), and also Jenness and Ballantyne mention *Chama* as material for shell discs in Goodenough (1920: p. 53).

I therefore asked the British Museum for an identification of the *kaloma* shell collected by Malinowski (shown in figure 15 in Cranstone 1961: p. 58). The specimen (reg. no. 1922 M 300) was then identified at the Natural History Department of the British Museum. It is a *Chama* species (D.C. Starzecka, personal communication). For two of the three sources of kula necklaces we can therefore establish that Malinowski was wrong.

The third case, that of necklaces coming from Port Moresby, is still unsolved. I suppose that Malinowski got the idea that shell discs were made out of *Spondylus* in Port Moresby, where he saw the manufacture of *ageva* (shell discs) in a Motu village (*ibid.* p. 506). According to Barton the *ageva* are made from *Spondylus* (in Seligmann 1910: p. 114n.). This may have been so. I do not know if shell discs are still made in that area.

It would, however, not be unlikely if different species of shell were used for kula necklaces, considering the range of colours 'from muddy brown to carmine red' the necklaces show (Malinowski 1922: p. 87).

With regard to the *mwali*, or armshells, it should be noted that *Conus millepunctatus* (Lamarck) is a synonym for *Conus leopardus* (Roding), the latter now the more accepted designation. Another *Conus*, *C. litteratus*, may probably also be used for the smaller armshells. Its size is 60-120 mm, while the *C. leopardus* is 120-220 mm.

Literature:

A good general guide to sea shells is S.P. Dance (ed.) *The Encyclopedia of Shells.* Blandford Press, London, 1974. The largest number of coloured illustrations of Pacific shells is found in T. Kira and T. Habe, *Shells of the Western Pacific in Colour.* 2 vols. Hoikusha Publ. Co., Osaka, 1962-1964.

JOHN LIEP

References:

Cranstone, B.A.L. (1961) *Melanesia: A Short Ethnography*. London.
Jenness, D. & Ballantyne, A. (1920) *The Northern D'Entrecasteaux*. Oxford.
Malinowski, B. (1922) *Argonauts of the Western Pacific*. London.
Seligmann, C.G. (1910) *The Melanesians of British New Guinea*. Cambridge.

Index of Authors

Abel, C.W.   63
Aceves, J.B.   122
Affleck, D.   64
Allen, J.   545
Anderson, I.   123
Andrew, Rev. J.R.   65
Anon.   45, 66, 84, 124–128
Arensberg, C.   67, 129
Armstrong, W.E.   130, 131
Austen, J.   68
Austen, L.   69, 132–136, 546
Baal, J. van   137
Badcock, C.R.   138
Bailey, F.G.   139
Balandier, G.   140
Baldwin, B.   57
Ballantyne, A.   141, 312–314
Baric, L.   142
Barnouw, V.   143
Barrow, T.   582, 588
Barth, F.   144
Bartlett, H.K.   583
Barton, F.R.   46, 145, 146
Beals, R.   147
Beier, U.   70–71, 97–98, 584, 585
Beledami, N.   72
Bell, F.   148
Belshaw, C.S.   149, 150–151
Benedict, R.   152
Berde, S.   73, 153–157
Besseignet, P.   158
Bevan, T.   74
Billy, T.   75
Birket-Smith, K.   159
Black, R.H.   76
Blau, P.M.   160–161
Boas, F.   162
Bock, P.K.   163
Bohannan, P.   164–165

Bowman, G.   166
Bradfield, R.M.   167
Brain, R.   168
British Museum   586–587
Bromilow, W.E.   77–80
Brookfield, H.C.   169–171
Brown, P.   172
Brunton, R.   173–174
Buettner-Janusch, J.   175, 444
Bühler, A.   588
Bunzel, R.   176
Burling, R.   177
Burnett, F.   81
Burns, T.   178
Burridge, K.   179
Campbell, S.   180–181
Carter, M.   182
Cassady, R.   183
Cayley-Webster, H.   82
Chapple, E.D.   184
Chowning, A.   185–189
Churchill, W.   547
Codere, H.   190–191
Cohen, P.S.   192
Collins, J.J.   193
Colson, E.   194
Cook, B.   619
Coon, C.S.   195
Cooper, M.   178, 196
Coppenhauer, D.   197
Couper, A.   198
Cranstone, B.A.I.   199
Crosby, E.   200, 548
Curti, P.A.   83
Dalton, G.   201–211
Damon, F.H.   212–214, 549
Dark, P.J.   589
De Waal Malefijt, A.   215
Dickson, T.E.   590–591

87

89